CU00759716

"If you want to know what is next in finance and
Lukomnik and Hawley expertly show how financia
limitations of that theory and what is poised to take
markets of the future."

— *Matt Orsagh*, Director of Capital Markets Policy, CFA Institute

"Lukomnik and Hawley provide an insightful case for the need to modernize
Modern Portfolio Theory. Investors, academics, and everyone interested in
finance and a sustainable future should read it – it will challenge how you
think!"

— *Caroline Flammer*, Associate Professor, Boston University and Chair,
PRI Academic Advisory Committee

"This definitive analysis of the limitations of Modern Portfolio Theory and the
gaps it has left behind is a must-read for anyone wishing to understand where
investment is now headed. It demonstrates why and how investment must
evolve in coming years and is the foundation on which forward-thinking
investors are now building a new practice."

— *Steve Lydenberg*, Founder and CEO, The Investment Integration Project

"Lukomnik and Hawley brilliantly make the point that Modern Portfolio
Theory is limited in its ability to deal with systemic risks that affect capital
markets, investors and society. They highlight the increasing realization that
investing success is inextricably linked to the health of the economy and capital
markets, rather than just to an investor's superior stock-picking prowess. They
show clearly how investors have moved beyond diversification to act on climate
change and other material ESG risks."

— *Sacha Sadan*, Director of Investment Stewardship, Legal and General
Investment Management

"At a time of deep reflection around the purpose of companies and financial
markets, *'Investing that Matters'* steers us towards a more enlightened view of
capitalism in the 21st century. It teaches us that long-term value creation is
achieved beyond simple analysis of a company's historical financial performance
and encourages the reader to appreciate the importance of deeper systemic risks
– ecological destruction, technological advancement and demographic shifts –
which will shape the corporate governance landscape as we know it. Lukomnik
and Hawley offer an important book, illuminating how modern portfolio
theory needs to evolve to better serve our economies and societies now and into
the future."

— *Kerrie Waring*, Chief Executive Officer, International Corporate
Governance Network

"Moving Beyond Modern Portfolio Theory is a highly needed book, in which
Jim and Jon realign finance with the real world, reminding us of its purpose.

I'm delighted we can now cite it and share it with students who feel a sense of confusion and distrust when they submit financial theories to their critical thinking, and with investors in search of a sense of purpose and impact. Portfolio and investing activity clearly affect the system – the financial, ecological, social world we live in. Jim and Jon make this argument very convincingly here, in a finance book that matters!"

— *Christel Dumas*, Associate Professor, ICHEC

"If you are puzzled by the current disconnect between the stock market and the real economy, but hopeful that investing can go back to its main purpose, that is allocating capital to address societal problems, you should read *Investing that Mattes*. An intelligent and accessible reflection on how Modern Portfolio Theory shaped the investing world we live today, and how it is now holding it back from addressing the challenges we face as a society. *Investing that Matters* suggests that practice is leading theory in experimenting with novel ways for investors to conceptualize and directly tackle systemic risk, through various forms of *Beta activism*. Still, our ability to theorize these practices is lagging. Calling for more active stewardship of investment to work on the root causes of risk, rather than playing with its statistical properties, the authors suggest the steps investors should take to take on this challenge."

— *Fabrizio Ferraro*, Professor and head of Strategic Management Department, IESE Business School

Moving Beyond Modern Portfolio Theory

Moving Beyond Modern Portfolio Theory: Investing That Matters tells the story of how Modern Portfolio Theory (MPT) revolutionized the investing world and the real economy, but is now showing its age. MPT has no mechanism to understand its impacts on the environmental, social, and financial systems, nor any tools for investors to mitigate the havoc that systemic risks can wreck on their portfolios. It is time for MPT to evolve.

The authors propose a new imperative to improve finance's ability to fulfil its twin main purposes: providing adequate returns to individuals and directing capital to where it is needed in the economy. They show how some of the largest investors in the world focus not on picking stocks, but on mitigating systemic risks, such as climate change and a lack of gender diversity, in order to improve the risk/return of the market as a whole, despite current theory saying that this should be impossible. "Moving beyond MPT" recognizes the complex relations between investing and the systems on which capital markets rely, "Investing that matters" embraces MPT's focus on diversification and risk adjusted return, but understands them in the context of the real economy and the total return needs of investors.

Whether an investor, an MBA student, a professor of finance or a sustainability professional, *Moving Beyond Modern Portfolio Theory: Investing That Matters* is thought-provoking and relevant. Its bold critique shows how the real world already is moving beyond investing orthodoxy.

Jon Lukomnik is the managing partner of Sinclair Capital LLC, a strategic consultancy to institutional investors, and a Senior Fellow at the High Meadows Institute.

James P. Hawley is Senior ESG Advisor, Truvalue Labs, a Factset Company. San Francisco, and Professor Emeritus School of Economics and Business, Saint Mary College of California.

Moving Beyond Modern Portfolio Theory

Investing That Matters

Jon Lukomnik and James P. Hawley

Routledge
Taylor & Francis Group

LONDON AND NEW YORK

First published 2021
by Routledge
2 Park Square, Milton Park, Abingdon, Oxon OX14 4RN

and by Routledge
52 Vanderbilt Avenue, New York, NY 10017

Routledge is an imprint of the Taylor & Francis Group, an informa business

© 2021 Jon Lukomnik and James P. Hawley

The right of Jon Lukomnik and James P. Hawley to be identified as authors
of this work has been asserted by them in accordance with sections 77 and 78
of the Copyright, Designs and Patents Act 1988.

All rights reserved. No part of this book may be reprinted or reproduced or
utilised in any form or by any electronic, mechanical, or other means, now
known or hereafter invented, including photocopying and recording, or in any
information storage or retrieval system, without permission in writing from
the publishers.

Trademark notice: Product or corporate names may be trademarks or
registered trademarks, and are used only for identification and explanation
without intent to infringe.

British Library Cataloguing-in-Publication Data
A catalogue record for this book is available from the British Library

Library of Congress Cataloging-in-Publication Data
A catalog record has been requested for this book

ISBN: 978-0-367-36995-8 (hbk)
ISBN: 978-0-367-76082-3 (pbk)
ISBN: 978-0-429-35225-6 (ebk)

Typeset in Sabon
by Taylor & Francis Books

Contents

Figures

Contributors

Jon Lukomnik is the managing partner of Sinclair Capital LLC, a strategic consultancy to institutional investors, and a Senior Fellow at the High Meadows Institute. He was the Pembroke Visiting Professor at the Judge Business School at Cambridge for the winter 2020 semester. He has been the investment advisor or a trustee for more than $100 billion (including New York City's pension funds). He has overseen more than 80 studies examining the capital markets. He is a member of the Deloitte Audit Quality Advisory Committee, and a trustee on the Van Eck mutual funds and European UCITs and a former member of the Standing Advisory Group of the Public Company Accounting Oversight Board. Jon has been honored by the International Corporate Governance Network, the Council of Institutional Investors, Ethisphere, the National Association of Corporate Directors (US), Transparency Task Force (UK), and Global Proxy Watch. His book, *The New Capitalists* (2006), was a "pick of the year" by the *Financial Times*.

James P. Hawley is Senior ESG Advisor, Truvalue Labs, a Factset company, and Professor Emeritus School of Economics and Business, Saint Mary College of California. He is the author or co-author of two books, the first on international banks and the global monetary system, and also of the influential *The Rise of Fiduciary Capitalism* (2001). He was co-editor of *Corporate Governance Failures: The role of institutional investors in the global financial crisis* (2011), as well as of *The Cambridge Handbook of Institutional Investment and Fiduciary Duty* (2014), and *The Routledge Handbook of Responsible Investment* (2015). He is the author (or co-author) of numerous scholarly articles and papers. He has been an invited guest professor at the Université de Paris, Université de Montpellier, Maastricht, and St. Gallen University. He has been a guest scholar at the Judge University (Business School) at Cambridge University, UK, and at the Kennedy School, Hauser Center, Initiative for Responsible Investment, Harvard University. He has spoken at numerous professional investor conferences and is frequently quoted in business and other media.

Acknowledgments

The authors would like to thank the following individuals who contributed ideas, critiques, and inspiration for this book: Constanza Consolandi, Stephen Davis, Christel Dumas, Caroline Flammer, Keith Johnson, Oguzhan Karakas, Steve Lydenberg, Harinder Mann, Ellen Quigley, David Pitt-Watson, Paul Rissman, Delilah Rothenberg, Judy Samuelson, Lord Chris Smith, and Demosthenes Tambakis.

We would also like to thank the following institutions for encouraging our research: Judge Business School (Cambridge University), High Meadows Institute, Pembroke College (Cambridge University), Pensions Insurance Corporation, and TruValue Labs.

We dedicate this book to Diane, Rebecca, Jesse, and Satya, and to Lynn, Julia, and Aidan.

Introduction

In the following pages we tell the story of how one financial theory – a Nobel Prize-winning theory accepted by almost everyone – enriched the world in the twentieth century but promises to diminish it in the twenty-first. We argue that Modern Portfolio Theory (MPT) and the investing philosophies built around it are showing their age. It is time to evolve. Such evolution is essential in order to improve and make sustainable finance's ability to fulfill its twin main purposes: Providing adequate risk adjusted returns to investors and directing capital to where it is needed in the economy.

Why should anyone not involved in the finance industry care about a financial theory? Consider that the capital markets affect which businesses thrive and which are starved of capital. Whether coal-fired power plants are funded or whether capital flows to renewable energy projects. Whether businesses extract value from society or add to it. Whether you will be able to retire in comfort, or in squalor. Whether diversity is valued or marginalized in the economy.

We estimate that some $100 trillion in capital is professionally managed across the globe. And virtually all of these investments are managed according to MPT tenets. This historically unprecedented concentration of ownership and capital in the hands of large institutional asset managers is the backdrop of our book. It was powered by, and now empowers, MPT. How and why it has outlived its usefulness is what we argue. How practice has outrun theory even while asset managers pledge allegiance to MPT is an irony that we examine.

Harry Markowitz won the Nobel Prize for inventing MPT in 1952 for good reason. His insights into the nature of diversification changed investing. It allowed the creation of index funds, facilitated the growth of mutual funds, enabled 401(k) funds in the USA, ISAs in the UK, and myriad retirement and other savings funds around the world. Perhaps most importantly, he justified investors taking calculated risks on a portfolio-wide basis, thereby allowing capital to flow to new endeavors that benefitted the economy and society.

MPT says that you can diversify many risks by creating a portfolio of stocks rather than just holding a few and choosing them only on their individual risk profile, as was typically the case before MPT. But MPT also argues that you cannot escape the impact of systemic risk generated by the social, environmental, and financial systems on your investments. Rather, you just have to accept the resultant systematic market risk, or "beta", as investors call it. (Throughout this book we distinguish between systematic risk, which we define as non-diversifiable risk to investments, and systemic or system risk, which is the risk to or arising from, environmental, social, or financial systems. Systemic risks often create non-diversifiable systematic risk.)

Whether caused by economic distress or climate change, MPT claims that beta will impact your portfolio, but that you cannot affect beta. This is what we call "The MPT paradox," which lies at MPT's very heart. There are two major elements to the paradox. The first is that innumerable studies prove that systematic risk affects your investment return some ten times more than your skill in picking securities or constructing diversified portfolios. Hence the first part of the paradox: MPT tells us that what you can affect is what matters least. The second part is that MPT is wrong about systematic risk: Yes, systematic risk affects portfolios, but, contrary to MPT, portfolios and investing activity also affect systematic risk. It is a symbiotic relation.

We argue that, contrary to MPT's assertion, the risks and returns of "the market" are affected by investors' decisions. Feedback loops abound. Despite MPT's widespread adherence, we show how investors affect systematic risk, both intentionally and unintentionally. That, in turn, suggests that deliberately adding a systems focus to MPT can mitigate many of the causes of system risk that in turn are inputs into systematic market risk. Although sudden shocks to the financial markets certainly do occur (the Covid-19 pandemic is a striking case in point), these often preventable surprises are fewer than generally thought and result from a lack of understanding or a failure of will, not from an inability to prevent, or at least to mitigate, them. For example, pandemic threats have been well known and widely studied.

We report how the largest investors in the world are trying to mitigate systemic risks, from climate change to lack of gender, ethnic, and racial diversity to the growth of anti-microbial resistant bacteria. Their actions speak more loudly than the drone of MPT traditionalists denying their ability to do so. We want to shine a spotlight on what is hiding in plain sight: That the biggest investors in the world have in practice evolved beyond the limitations of current theory (which, ironically, the majority think that they still practice) in ways that fundamentally affect the economy, the environment, and the social conventions by which we all live.

To our knowledge, this is the first book to suggest that these real-world non-MPT actions form a coherent challenge to one of MPT's central tenets rather than being a series of isolated incidents. Many of these actions focus on systemic risk. The ability to mitigate systemic risk changes almost everything. It means that improving the overall market return is both more powerful than beating that market return through security selection and that it is necessary and possible to do so. It means that much of today's focus on relative performance is actually myopic, because focusing on system health (which cannot be benchmarked on a relative basis) over the long term will positively impact financial and economic returns more. And it portends a powerful new force in the fight against global warming, income inequality, gender, ethnic, and racial discrimination, and other systemic risks that threaten to depress returns, not to mention disrupt society.

MPT treats investing as a bloodless discipline, divorced from real-world messes like financial crises, income inequality, and global warming. By contrast, our approach understands that there are causal relationships and feedback loops between investments and the environmental, social, and financial systems on which the capital markets, and we as human beings, depend.

This is what we mean by our title and sub-title of the book. "Investing that matters," because investing is and should be linked to the twin purposes of investing, which is to allocate capital efficiently to the real non-financial economy and society and to provide a real and risk-controlled return to people, now and in the future. "Moving Beyond Modern Portfolio Theory," because MPT and much financial theory has lost track of its origins in and its actual links to the political economy in which it lives, and from which is sprung. Reuniting finance with the broader economy is vital for society, but critical also for finance itself. *Moving Beyond Mordern Portfolio Theory* ties all those threads together and suggests a conceptual frame to facilitate action. That is our motivation for this book.

1 The MPT Revolution Devours Its Children

The MPT Revolution Devours Its Children

Modern Portfolio Theory (MPT) changed the investing world and financial markets. It changed the world's economy. It was nothing less than a revolution. But, as French journalist Jacques Mallet du Pan observed at the time of the French Revolution, "Like Saturn, the revolution devours its children."

Du Pan's analogy fits. In the Greek myth to which he refers, Saturn – or Cronus in the original Greek – was the Titan who ruled the Earth for eons. Warned by prophecy that one of his six children will supplant him, Cronus attempted to swallow them all. However, Zeus survived and fulfilled the prophecy, defeating Cronus and the Titans, ushering in the golden age of the Olympian Gods.

MPT is the financial markets' Cronus, a powerful theoretical framing of how investing should work. It has been successful for generations. It has reassured investors who want certainty about complex market behavior, just as Cronus reassured the ancients about the workings of the complex world. But MPT has become old. It faces not just one threat to its dominance but three. First, it is a victim of its own success, much the way that Cronus's own fertility sowed the seeds of his downfall. Second, capital markets have changed in ways that Harry Markowitz, the father of MPT, could not have foreseen when he wrote his seminal paper in 1952. Capital markets have matured, as Zeus did, into a force that overwhelms some of the assumptions upon which MPT was built. Finally, just as Cronus was the ruler of a world built around the Titans but could not escape from his prophesied fate, so, too, MPT cannot escape from its origin as a way to diversify idiosyncratic risk and its inability to provide a framework for mitigating systematic risks. Indeed, MPT does not even try. That is a fateful error of omission. It laid the groundwork for multiple generations to view investing as somehow separate and apart from – and having no role in – mitigating risks to the financial, social, and environmental systems on which the capital markets rely. Thus, the MPT tradition fails doubly from errors of omission: first by ignoring that systematic risk can be influenced and mitigated; and second by ignoring the link between systematic risk and systemic (system) risk. (NB: Throughout this book, we use systematic risk to denote risks that originate from the same source and affect a broad swath of securities. We use systemic risk for risks to the economic, social and financial systems on which the capital markets depend, and which affect those systems, such as the 2020 Covid-19 pandemic or the 2008 financial crisis.)

Whether the issue is 2020's coronavirus pandemic, 2008's financial crisis, or the ongoing risks of climate change and income inequality, capital markets and society alike increasingly recognize that MPT's essential revolutionary development – the ability to diversify idiosyncratic risk – is limited when faced with non-diversifiable systematic risks. MPT's ability to produce desirable risk-adjusted returns and to efficiently allocate capital when non-diversifiable risks affect markets, economies, and society is puny. Even in non-crisis times, idiosyncratic risk is only a marginal contributor to the overall risk/return profile of any investor's portfolio and is becoming increasingly more marginal as computing power and research define more and more systematic risk factors. This is due to the insight and practice of MPT itself: to the degree that idiosyncratic risk is diversified away, idiosyncratic risk can in theory be reduced to zero. However, systematic and systemic risks matter more – much more, than idiosyncratic risks, but MPT provides no tool to mitigate them, either for investors or for society. Indeed, Markowitz and the MPT tradition which build upon his ideas were not and are not focused on this; some even deny that it can or should be done. In effect, MPT focuses on that which matters least – a phenomenon that we call the MPT paradox. That is a key focus of chapter two. But before exploring MPT's original sin, we should understand how revolutionary MPT has been, critiques of the assumptions behind the theory, and the theories which build on MPT, and why it has become a victim of its own success. That is the focus of this chapter.

Before Markowitz and MPT

Before the second half of the twentieth century, investment risk analysis (and therefore risk measurement and management) focused on the individual security. For example, central government bonds were (and still are) considered "safe", initial public offerings of small company stocks relying on an unproven business model were (and still should be) considered "risky", and more established companies' issues were analyzed on their own individual merits. And that was pretty much it.

Although the investing universe was smaller and the focus was on asset by asset risk analysis, there was significant (and long-lasting) debate between those who, like Graham and Dodd, focused on value and fundamental investing vis–à-vis individual stocks but had no coherent theory about how to create a portfolio and those who, like John Maynard Keynes, focused on the more psychological element of the stock market (the madness, or depending on one's view, wisdom of crowds). Graham and Dodd even made the pre-MPT case that the average institutional manager could not obtain better results than an index[1], (even though practical index funds were not yet available). What was missing for the adherents of both schools of thought was a coherent theory of how to invest. Followers of Graham and Dodd analyzed and picked securities but lacked a plan for their investments as a whole. Followers of Keynes focused on business cycles and market dynamics, but not how to translate those observations into a portfolio of securities.

Enter Harry Markowitz, a brilliant mathematician who also showed an intuitive understanding of what investors wanted and needed. Markowitz wrote in the very first paragraph of his 1952 paper: "...the investor does (or should) consider expected return a desirable thing and variance of return an undesirable thing."[2] Two key elements are captured in this sentence. The first is that Markowitz's perspective is purposively normative ("should"), rather than objectively descriptive ("does") of how markets actually work. Second, MPT distills the impact of all the causes of risk to a single metric: Volatility. As far as MPT is concerned, all risks – no matter the root cause – are reduced to their ability to create uncertainty around the future price of an asset. The root causes of any risk are largely irrelevant, except to the extent that the specifics cause the variance to correlate, which would cause directional co-movement and increase volatility in a portfolio of assets, or if not correlated, reduce volatility.

MPT's great leap forward was to define an investor's purpose as creating a "least mean variance" portfolio. That is, creating a portfolio designed to shrink the "wrongness" of an investor's guess as to future expected returns. MPT codified the job of an investor as maximizing return per unit of risk (or, conversely, reducing the risk per unit of return) by providing both a theory and the math to do so.

While diversification is not new – Miguel de Cervantes wrote "don't put all your eggs in one basket" in his masterpiece Don Quixote in 1615[3] – what Markowitz midwifed into the world in 1952 was ground-breaking all the same. The mathematics of his theory enabled investors to take individual assets that they might have shunned previously as "too risky" and reengineer those assets into something where the whole was more than the sum of its parts. MPT argues that the aggregate risk of the portfolio – not of the individual securities – is what matters, and that risk will inevitably be lower than that of the individual assets (as the returns on some of them will zig, while others zag, thereby dampening the price volatility of the portfolio overall).

These ideas, and their mathematical proofs, turned out to be exciting thoughts for an investor. If you were an investor previously limited to securities with a certain risk profile, you could now invest in riskier assets which provide higher expected returns. If you could blend them into a portfolio, with the price movement of the components imperfectly correlated, you could be fairly confident that the overall portfolio would return more than your previous allocation to less volatile investments, even while having the same or lower risk. Markowitz provided the theory and the proofs of how diversification enabled extra return without an investor "paying" for it by accepting extra risk.

One key result of MPT's wholesale adoption was that investors, newly freed from the constraints of buying only "safer" investments, focused on understanding the risk and return patterns of individual securities and other assets. Blending them into less volatile portfolio return patterns became the holy grail. Soon everyone was, and to a large extent still is, drinking from the MPT trough to create efficient portfolios.

The reaction of investors – even massive institutional investors – to MPT was tectonic. Let's look at just one example, although admittedly a trillion-dollar-plus example. In the US, public pension plans provide defined benefit pensions to literally tens of millions of public sector retirees and have trillions of dollars in aggregate asset. (There are also public sector defined contribution plans, and some sponsoring jurisdictions offer both.) For the history of these funds, until MPT, state legislatures restricted the types of securities that could be owned. For example, stocks were considered risky and often prohibited. Instead, pension funds typically were required to invest in fixed income investments, and often bonds which carried the full faith and credit or the United States, or which met certain credit tests. That depressed returns, but it was the primary form of risk control. Only in 1996 in the US did the states of Indiana, West Virginia, and South Carolina, the last states to have such restrictions, end the prohibition against their pension funds investing in stocks.[4] It took almost a half-century, but MPT finally conquered even the most conservative of state legislatures, as they saw their states' pension funds falling behind their peers and the low returns becoming a burden on their taxpayers. With the rise of MPT's more holistic portfolio theory, all states now have adopted some form of diversification as the law, theoretically anchored in MPT. Even the states that still have some type of restrictions by security type have raised the limits on the amount of "riskier" securities allowed, by creating "basket clauses" to which the legal limits do not apply, thereby creating de facto MPT investment regimes (e.g. New York State).[5]

That same sort of evolution, from looking at risk on a security by security basis to looking at portfolio risk, took place around the world. Indeed, the US public pension plan example is notable precisely because the political environment that governs those plans slowed the MPT investing revolution compared to most everywhere else. By the time of the last states' adoption in 1996, MPT was the justification for just about every regulation about allowable securities in collective investment plans around the world. The fact that MPT could change not just market participants' ideas of how to manage risk, but also lawmakers (at least some of whom are skeptical of financial innovation), demonstrates just how omnipresent MPT has become.

What was needed to unlock diversification's power was numbers, computational power, and resulting analytics. If an investor knows the expected return, expected volatility, and expected correlation of the assets in his or her portfolio, he or she can create the least mean variance portfolio for a desired level of return or, to put it another way, the highest-returning portfolio for a specified level of risk. (We are frequently amazed that the tautology implied in the theory is not more frequently remarked upon: In order to predict the future, an investor needs to have a prediction of what elements of the future will look like. Of course, if an investor could predict the future of risk-free rates, that investor would be foolish to have a diversified portfolio. He or she would be better off picking the single asset or a few assets with the actual best return(s) for the desired period of investment.)

It is worth noting that MPT's math is somewhat sealed away from the real world. MPT constrains investors to the role of observers of the portfolio companies in which they invested. MPT's focus on price variability in the financial markets – and not on value creation in the real economy – was a step along the path that separated markets from the real economy, as it creates barriers between capital and active ownership.[6] Even what we call investors – "analysts" and "portfolio managers" – reflects the divide between MPT's view of the real economy and the capital markets. Investors *analyze* real-world companies but *manage* portfolios of financial assets. This divide relegates the purposes of finance – such as intermediation (allocation of capital) and the creation of a risk-adjusted return where risk is measured relative to the real-world liabilities – to far corners of conversation and study, where it has remained until after the 2008 financial crisis.[7]

To be a good investor in the MPT construct means creating the most efficient portfolio, thereby squeezing the maximum return out of each unit of risk. Investors able to do this prospered. Compared with the overall market average, they coaxed extra returns from their portfolio for the amount of risk (volatility) undertaken.

Following the introduction of the Capital Asset Pricing Model (see below), Investors called this excess return "alpha". (Technically excess return is not the same as Jensen's alpha, in that alpha requires similar risk profiles of the specific portfolio and the comparison portfolio. However, in practice, excess return and alpha tend to be used interchangeably.) Interestingly, though excess return can be positive or negative, and for most time periods most portfolios minus fees lag the overall market, the phrase "excess" return semantically suggests a positive skew. But excess to what? The answer: To the risk/return profile of the entire market, or what investors call "beta". Technically, alpha is the residual return not able to be explained by a portfolio's "beta"[8] – that is, the return to systematic risk, as we discuss below. (As with alpha, there is a technical definition of beta: a measure of a portfolio's or individual security's relative volatility to the market as a whole. The "market" gets assigned a beta of 1.0. Securities, or sets of securities, or entire asset classes have betas relative to the market. For instance, a small cap growth stock would typically have a beta of greater than 1.0, indicating more volatility than the general market, whereas a large cap utility stock would typically have a beta of less than 1.0.)

However, soon a de facto market semantic developed. Positive excess return against a benchmark was called alpha, and portfolio managers often attributed those positively skewed returns to their skill. (Perhaps not surprisingly, negative alpha, or the negative return not attributable to the beta of a portfolio, is often just called risk by the very same investors, in a semantic variance of the "heads I win, tails you lose" game.)

To some degree, this makes sense. The market is in effect the opportunity set of securities from which an investor can select to create a portfolio, so measuring return relative to the market serves to measure the skill of the portfolio's creator. Moreover, the efficient market hypothesis (discussed below) suggests that the risk/return profile of the market is the product of the wisdom of all investors, which would seem to be a fair benchmark against which to judge any investor's ability to under- or out-perform.

Soon the rules of how to "win" at MPT became apparent: The market's risk and return are the standards against which its components – the individual securities that compose the overall market – are compared. Conventions arose; for example, setting the overall market's beta at 1.0, and measuring each individual security's beta relatively to the market. Riskier securities, in terms of volatility, have betas of more than 1.0, less risky securities betas of less than 1.0.

Being able to "beat the benchmark" became the goal, which had the remarkable, although rarely remarked upon, effect of changing the goal of a "good" investor from meeting his or her needs in the real world, to beating the market's returns. Stock-pickers like Peter Lynch at Fidelity's Magellan fund or Bill Miller at Legg Mason, who appeared to be able to do so consistently, became stars, standing astride the financial markets the way the Titans used to surmount the ancient world. As it turns out, both the ancient Titans – and the titans of the markets – were products of their times. They both were successful at ruling their worlds. But worlds change. And new myths emerge while old ones are debunked.

Assumptions, Hypotheses and Myths: The Growth of the MPT Tradition

Let's look at the critical assumptions and hypotheses underlying MPT, as well as the post-Markowitz theories which have become part of the MPT tradition. We also will examine a number of the important criticisms of those theories, assumptions, and arguments. Then we will look at the evolution of markets and investors since Markowitz, resulting in a changed landscape that lays bare the inevitability of investment theory moving beyond MPT. Finally, we will examine how MPT, like Cronus, has sown the seeds of its own decline.

(ir)Rational Actors, (ir)Rational Markets

In his 1990 Nobel Prize lecture, Markowitz argued that "the theory of rational choice under uncertainty" is a necessary complement to MPT. In other words, the assumption (or perhaps argument) that the market is, or should be, composed of rational actors is an essential element of MPT.[9]

Markowitz meant rational in the technical economic sense, meaning that investors will always select from a set of choices the one which will maximize utility, defined for MPT as risk-adjusted return. It is important to note that Markowitz argued not that investors were rational in fact, but rather that they should be: The theory was explicitly normative, prescriptive and as Donald MacKenzie argues "performative."[10] That is, to the degree that MPT was believed and acted upon, it created its own reality. It was a great strength of MPT that over time it shaped how market actors functioned, and thus how markets came to be structured and how they operated. To the degree that investors and money managers could be convinced of the performance and power of MPT (and thus act on it), MPT would prove its worth; particularly in the low-concentrated markets dominated by relatively small investors as existed in the 1950s into the 1980s in the USA, the UK, and some other countries.[11] Although Markowitz himself did not focus much on what became known as rational expectations theory, MPT can in fact be seen as an attempt to make portfolios more rational by defining the utility function against which rationality can be judged. Projecting outward and forward, an MPT lens applied broadly by investors would push markets toward rationality, too.

The rational actor assumption and prescription of MPT is a reflection of the larger economics profession's schools of thought, a major strain of which came to explicitly assume, for the sake of an increasingly mathematized vision of economics, *homo economicus* – that is, the hypothesized calculating, rational, utility maximizing "economic human."[12]

The rational actor assumption often leads to a rational market assumption. That certainly was not always the case. Keynes, for example, argued that the stock market (in which he was heavily personally invested) was more akin to a casino than a rational marketplace, in that crowd psychology is important, and events are not therefore random. Rather, one act depends on and is related to another (a forerunner of an important criticism of the "random walk" hypothesis). That meant that neither individual judgements nor markets were always rational. This is illustrated by his famous English newspaper beauty contest example, where contestants do not judge the beauty of the women, but rather bet on how others judge her, resulting in an endless loop process.[13] Opposed to Keynes was his contemporary, Irving Fisher, who argued strongly for rational markets.[14] Fisher was hardly alone in the search for and theorizations of rational markets. In France, Bachelier (following his teacher, Henri Poincaré) examined stock prices as probabilities following a random bell curve, although Bachelier had the insight that while such random events (one not being dependent on the next) might apply to natural events (as in physics), human interaction make events less than random. This too often forgotten insight became revived in a widespread way following the 2008 financial crisis. Hyman Minsky developed similar insights focusing on the non-random linkages in speculative bubbles inherent in financial markets, as they are linked to the non-financial economy. Thus, although the debate is hardly new, what was striking about the second half of the twentieth century was how dominant rational actor/rational market models and assumptions became.

There are at least two obvious problems with the rational actor/rational markets model. First, it clearly is not aligned with the real-world of human behavior, including economic and financial behavior, as we will see. Second, it is the backbone of MPT. Furthermore, even if this assumption/argument fit the theoretical mold that Milton Friedman argued did not need to be correct or "truth" as long as "it worked", our (and many others') readings of the historical evidence is that it does not work currently, even if a plausible argument could be made that it more or less worked under some historical conditions.[15]

While rational humans and the related conception of rational expectations theory[16] dominated in most economics and finance academic departments for much of the last half century with significant practical implications, there was always a minority who pushed back. Even at the time, Herbert Simon stood out, arguing that most people, including those in key economic decision-making positions, have neither the time nor the talent to be entirely rational, in particular when it comes to information content and analysis. Well before the 1970s, Simon argued that key decision-makers were "satisficing" (satisfy and suffice), that is, taking short cuts and following rules of thumb (heuristics) rather than optimizing rational behavior. Rationality was, in his semantic, bounded rationality.[17]

Without getting into the (interesting) weeds of the relationships between (ir)rational actors and (ir)rational markets, it is useful to note that arguments were made about whether markets could and did take even irrational or bounded rational actions by market participants and still create rational outcomes. That is, could markets encompass irrational behaviors but themselves be "outcome rational" nonetheless, as there would be a tendency for the irrational behaviors to either a) be randomly distributed, thereby cancelling each other out, and allowing the "rational" central tendency to dominate, or b) for the irrationality to cease over time and for the market to come to its senses? Burton Malkiel (see below) is among those who argue that the market will, over time, become rational. The issues of why irrationality would be randomly distributed, or of how long could markets accommodate irrationality before becoming rational, and what "colleterial damage" that accommodation and reversion would cause – to markets themselves, as well as to the economy and society, as evidenced by the tech bubble at the turn of the century or the 2008 financial crisis – are not usually addressed by rational actor/rational market advocates.[18]

Random Walks Through Efficient Markets

Economic rationality is the core myth that MPT just cannot live without or escape. The *ideé fixe* of MPT, it becomes a key building block for ever more assumptions with ever more ramifications for investing and markets. Two key ones are random walk asset pricing and efficient markets. As New York University Professor Thomas Sargent notes: "Economists have used the concept of rational expectations to understand a variety of situations in which speculation about the future is a crucial factor in determining current action. Rational expectations are a building block for the 'random walk' or 'efficient markets' theory of securities prices..."[19]

Burton Malkiel is perhaps the best-known advocate for random walk/efficient pricing. In his best-seller, "A Random Walk Down Wall Street," Malkiel does not argue that all actions are based on rational expectations/rational "man" assumptions. Rather, he argues that over time the market ultimately discounts irrational actions. He writes: "Abnormalities can crop up [in markets] and often they attract unwary [non rational] investors. But, eventually, true value is recognized..." He continues: "Forecasts are invariably incorrect...risk is never clearly perceived, so the appropriate rate at which the future should be discounted is never certain."[20] His argument about rationality is that no single person or institution can consistently know more than the market in total (implying that no one investor can consistently outperform the market). The implicit assumption here is that the market over time finds the "correct" value of a given security and of the overall market. But at any moment, or for a time period, the market could be wrong, either overall, or with regard to a specific security's price. Yet temporality is critical, and in our view undercuts the argument that in fact the market is a random walk. This was recognized by Bachelier as the problem of averages and the long term: while modeling stochastic stock prices (random walks) he noted that in human affairs things were often affected by human/knowledge linkages, and thus may not be random but interactive. Bachelier's random walk claims were extremely short term, as only in the short term could one assume that each move was random (a coin toss) and critically, independent of the prior move, again as in a coin toss. As Poincaré noted, human decision-making is not a coin toss, as people react to prior and contemporary decisions of other humans.[21] Neither random nor independent over time was something that Bachelier readily acknowledged, even if his followers appear to have forgotten this major caveat.

We might add that averages (at a moment in time or over time) are somewhat akin the person who has one foot in scalding water and the other in ice water: The average is nice, but irrelevant. Similar too therefore are what Malkiel speaks of as "abnormalities" or irrational swings in the market. They can and do create real damage, such that the value-seeking average might not be relevant. The 2008 financial crisis is an obvious case in point. More generally, any purely "rational" investor, who seeks to take advantage of the market's "abnormalities" caused by "unwary (non-rational)" investors risks falling afoul of the famous warning that "the market can stay irrational longer than you can remain solvent."[22]

Rationality and random walk theory assume away financial intersectionality (the prices of unrelated securities influencing one another) and "path dependency" (the past influencing the present), as well as the Keynesian view of market psychology, which included both causes of non-randomness.

The well-known market dynamic between liquidity and price is one example of non-randomness, caused by financial intersectionality. In a crisis, when many investors must raise cash, it is often the most liquid non-impaired assets which are sold first, creating downward price pressure, which then impairs those same assets. In times of credit pressure, for instance, it is often government bonds that are sold first by bond investors, as the bids for the impaired below-investment-grade bonds (or mortgages, or asset-backed securities) disappear. Rather than sell the impaired securities at what they regard as fire-sale prices, investors will often raise cash by selling government bonds – or whatever is liquid. The result is price pressure on non-impaired securities in a distinctly non-random, non-rational way, as the price pressure on one set of securities affects others. Similarly, a problem in the equity or bond market of one "emerging market" may cause emerging market investors to sell the securities in what had been a different perfectly healthy market. This market contagion phenomenon, wherein one market or set of securities affects another, makes market price directionality predictable and non-random. The random walk assumption ignores the fact that the owners of securities have needs and liabilities. In effect, random walk theory, like MPT itself, assumes that financial markets − and the participants therein − are somehow sealed off from the real world and that what goes on in one market, or with one security, or even with the economy generally, will not affect other securities and markets.

Ironically, one of the three key Markowitzian capital market assumptions itself suggests how wrong that is and how powerful a force is financial inter-sectionality. During crises and market dislocations, investors often bemoan the fact that "correlations go to one," meaning that the prices of seemingly unrelated assets move in tandem.

Another problem with random walk is that prices are at least somewhat path-dependent. History might not repeat itself, but when it comes to pricing, past can be prologue to the present. As far back as 1993, two UCLA academics showed that path dependency mattered: They demonstrated that what has become known as a momentum strategy − buying stocks that had recently performed well and selling those that had performed poorly − resulted in abnormal positive returns for up to a year.[23] A number of other strategies with varying levels of real-world effectiveness − for example, trend following com-modity strategies and chart-based investing in many markets − also rely on past pricing and path-dependency. Every time you hear someone talk about a "resistance level" or "support", that is an attack on random walk theory.

The Capital Asset Pricing Model

What we call the MPT tradition builds on Markowitz, but over time is increasingly diverse in theories and practices. The first major breakthrough in the MPT tradition was the development of the Capital Asset Pricing Model (CAPM) by four academics, all working separately: William Sharpe and John Lintner in 1964 and 1965, respectively, and Jack Treynor and Jan Mossin all developed versions of CAPM. Simply put, CAPM says that the expected return of an asset is the risk-free rate of return, plus the product of the equity risk premium multiplied by the beta of that specific security (measured on a relative return basis compared with the market).[24] In other words, CAPM says that the expected return is directly related to how volatile is the asset as measured by its specific beta. The theory is that you are paid for taking risk, or, to put in in the inverse − an issuer of a security will have to pay more to attract investors to a riskier asset.

CAPM set out to address how to assess risk in the cost of capital, which had not previously been clearly conceptualized. Risk was based on Markowitz's mean variance formulation, with CAPM developers asking the question what if all investors follow the same advice of Markowitz's efficient frontier? That is, CAPM was, like MPT, normative. The hypothetical "if all investors follow the same advice" implies that the market is in equilibrium, meaning that each investor can and does determine the expected return as a function of risk.[25] Malkiel puts it this way: Before CAPM "it was believed that the return from a security varied with the variability or standard deviation of the returns it produced. [CAPM]...says that the total risk of each individual security is irrelevant. It is only the systematic component that counts as far as extra rewards go."[26]

CAPM adds two new assumptions to MPT, according to Fama and French. The first – the equilibrium assumption – is that for investors there is complete agreement that the market clears all asset prices. The second assumption of the CAPM model is that all investors have access to unlimited funds at the risk-free rate. We have already examined two other questionable assumptions on which MPT, and therefore CAPM rely – the efficient markets hypothesis and the idea of rational investors based on the *homo economicus* model. While it has long been understood that these simplifying assumptions mean CAPM does not explain reality, "the CAPM formula is still widely used because it is simple and allows for easy comparisons of investment alternatives."[27]

CAPM operationalized MPT, as it drastically simplified the calculations necessary. Markowitz's MPT required a risk calculation for each and every investment entity, whereas CAPM did not. It was argued that although it was inaccurate, it was accurate enough.[28] In this sense, CAPM is, like MPT, performative: People use the model to price securities (or, at least as a starting point to do so), and so it has power because it is used, not because it is correct.

Risk for CAPM is determined in the beta of assets, that is, its volatility variance compared with the market's volatility. As Bernstein quotes Perold: "...a risk that can be diversified away when held along with other investments in a portfolio is, in a very real way, not a risk at all."[29] That is, risk is systematic risk. MPT and CAPM recognized one factor: Non-diversifiable market beta. However, the subsequent the history of CAPM is a history of the increasing discovery of factors. Thus, Fama-French first find three, then five factors: e.g. size, book/market ratio, profitability. So-called smart beta investing includes the insights of MPT and CAPM's operationalization of it, but in the process of testing for and selecting from a host of factors essentially undercuts both MPT and CAPM assumptions. As at the time of writing, smart beta draws on 382 possible factors.[30] CAPM can be both normative and performative, but, as with MPT, theory has been bypassed by practice.[31]

Loss Versus Risk

More recently, another school of economics very much not in the MPT tradition has examined not what investors "should" do (per Markowitz) or what academics should think investors and markets should act "as if" because it works (per Friedman) or even bounded rationality (per Simon). Rather, behavioral economists researched how real-world investors actually behave. Daniel Kahneman was awarded the Nobel Prize for his and Amos Twersky's work on prospect theory, which proved investors are not, in the economic sense, rational. (Most people believe Twersky would have shared the prize, except that the prize is only given to living people.) Their work pioneered behavioral economics – an entire field devoted to understanding just how "irrational" investors and markets are. In other words, to understand how living, breathing *homo sapiens* makes economic decisions, rather than postulating a new *homo economicus* species.

Remember, the goal of Markowitzian MPT is to optimize risk-adjusted returns. That implies both economic rationality and risk-aversion as the dominant motivation. Kahneman and Twersky examined how people actually invest. They found that rather than thinking about a Markowitzian utility function of risk-adjusted return maximization, investors actually care about what they have, and what they can lose. In other words, they are loss averse, not risk-averse. In effect, investors manifest the old saying that a bird in the hand is worth two in the bush. In brief, they argue that people tend to underweight outcomes that are probabilistic as compared with perceived certainty. From this flow a host of other propositions which challenge utility theory, the foundation of both rational actor and rational expectation arguments.[32] This implies there are not necessarily proportional arithmetic trade-offs between choices that may result in loss or gain.

Prospect theory is also persuasive evidence of path dependency, rather than random walk behavior. After all, if investors are loss averse rather risk-averse then the price at which an asset was acquired matters. Whereas the Markowitzian risk-aversion motivation requires an opinion of the future and rationality, behavioralists' loss-aversion motivation requires knowledge of previous purchase/sale decisions and path-dependency.

Information and the Efficient Market Hypothesis: A Problematic Interplay

Although the efficient market hypothesis (EMH) was formulated by a number of leading economists coming to it from slightly different angles, the commonality is an assumption that the future is random, and that although at any given moment markets might not act rationally by overshooting or undershooting, overvaluing or undervaluing, or merely hovering around a statistical equilibrium, they will correct. A key element in EMH's argumentation (or perhaps more accurately, its assumption) is that information flows into prices (and, in the strongest formulation of EMH, instantly, without friction, and evenly across the marketplace). Yet evidence is weak, as is the logic.[33]

As Gilson and Kraakman argued, a key weakness of the EMH is specifying conceptually and proving empirically the exact process(es) by which information affects prices. This is of course not a financial question as such, but rather a question of human comprehension, technology, media, and information theory. Two types of market efficiency transmission mechanisms are often articulated: Information efficiency and fundamental value efficiency.

Information efficiency is typically defined to mean that a trader cannot beat the market because the market has already incorporated material information into price. As with the other assumptions behind EMH and MPT, information efficiency is an attractive proposition in that it simplifies analysis and provides consistency to models. But it is not borne out by reality. One critical problem is that information efficiency assumes that all active market participants are price-takers. That might have been true in 1952, when Markowitz wrote his thesis. But the higher level of market participant concentration today means that large investors can be price makers (at least some of the time), leveraging their market power. Other market evolutions, including technological innovations, also result in challenges to the idea of information efficiency. For example, computers co-located in exchange-trading centers seek to reduce "latency" – that is, the delay in the dissemination of sensitive pricing information owing to the time that it takes to transmit it over distances. That latency is measured in milliseconds, but it is enough to give those high-frequency traders with co-located computers an informational advantage. High-frequency traders of the early twenty-first[t] century and the investors of today who scrape Twitter feeds for market-moving information all recognize the value in having information sooner than the rest of the market, in violation of the information efficiency assumption. If information efficiency were really a fundamental feature of capital markets, rather than a simplifying assumption, there would be no need for insider trading laws designed to even the playing field as much as possible. Such laws implicitly recognize that true, market-wide information efficiency is an unachievable goal.

While market concentration and technologic challenges to information efficiency might be considered *ex post* developments which were not contemporaneous with the development of the efficient market hypothesis, the fact is that another pesky fact made clear that information efficiency never existed. Simply put, arbitrage existed then. It is elegant for EMH proponents to say that markets self-correct over time. The implication is that each pricing anomaly that gives rise to an arbitrage opportunity is a one-off, quickly corrected, rather than a set of anomalies that are a permanent (or at least semi-permanent) feature of markets. But the self-correction postulate must, therefore, assume a virtually inexhaustible supply of arbitrage opportunities which are extinguished *ad seriatim* and relatively quickly, but replaced by new ones that the market has not yet seen. But some arbitrage opportunities are remarkably sticky and persist over time. They might come to an end eventually, but they last for years, which is long enough for to wonder which is the temporary condition and which is the permanent one: Inefficient markets with pricing anomalies or perfectly priced efficient markets. One example of sticky market arbitrage that lasted for decades was convertible bond arbitrage (and more generally capital structure arbitrage), which relied on the inefficient transmittal of information between the stock and bond markets.

The second type of efficiency is fundamental value efficiency. This belief is that not only does the market respond quickly and accurately to information, but that the price of a security actually reflects its economic value (that is, for example, its discounted cash flow).[34] This assumes that information leads in an unmediated way to knowing and knowing to acting. To the contrary, most information science suggests that information necessitates interpretation, meaning differences are inevitable and actions based on the same "information" will be diverse.

Put a bit differently, Malkiel writes: "...the argument here is that the structure of market prices already takes into account any public information that may be contained in balance sheets, income statement...[such that] analysis of these data will be useless."[35] Given the number of accountants and accounting firms and what they charge, and the number of analysts employed by asset owners and managers, one must wonder how this information comes to be, full blown form Zeus's head? Indeed, one also wonders why there is so much disagreement ("reasonable people can differ")? The efficient market assumption itself relies on these two assumptions: that all information is knowledge, and all information is known, or mostly known. Yet information is not knowledge, and most knowledge involves judgment, meaning that it is never a sure thing. Nonetheless, Malkiel argues that EMH does not claim that prices are always right, but rather that nobody can know whether they are too high or too low. Rather, EMH implies that information is absorbed so efficiently, and that information (events) are so random (statistically) that one cannot buy or sell fast enough.[36] This statement conflates two entirely different thoughts. The first is that no individual knows more than the market (although the market itself may not be "right"). The second is that the market ("wisdom of crowds") absorbs information, but it is considered random because nobody can predict what information will appear and/or what effect it will have on price.[37] The first might be correct, but it does not follow that information is always baked into prices unless one assumes a total efficient absorption and comprehension process of "information."

In fact, there is evidence that the opposite is true: Having "better" information and analysis was so consistent and lucrative a phenomenon during the heyday of Markowitz and Malkiel that large investment banks capitalized elite units with the express purpose of taking advantage of price anomalies caused by informational asymmetries around fundamental value. Robert Rubin famously rode the success of Goldman Sachs' risk arbitrage desk to a position atop Goldman and then to being the Treasury Secretary of the United States. Along the way he mentored a host of future hedge fund titans who also practiced risk and statistical arbitrage (as well as traditional active security selection).[38] Structural impediments to fundamental value efficiency persist. For example, many institutional investors are limited to investing on in investment grade bonds. When a bond is downrated to "junk bond" status, they must sell the bonds, creating a market dislocation. This information is well known, and other investors specialize in buying these so-called "fallen angel" bonds. But the persistence of the pricing anomaly suggests that the information continues to be inefficiently absorbed by the market in setting prices.

Even for a theoretical model, the assumption of a relatively even and rapid dissemination of information effectively and efficiently determining prices is a heroic assumption.

As a normative or perhaps performative theory, MPT needed rationality, rational markets, random walks, and the efficient market hypothesis not because they were objectively correct, but because they each reinforced the normative framework of MPT and made the math work. Without efficient markets there would be no basis against which to reasonably analyze mean-variance and therefore no meaningful way to know how to structure a portfolio in order to optimize risk and return. The theories describe investors and capital markets as the theoreticians wished them to be, rather than as they are.

There is a huge literature about the investor rationality, market rationality, information efficiency, random walks, and the efficient market hypothesis. Our purpose in setting out the above was not a comprehensive literature review, but rather to suggest that, in some ways, they were always a set of inductive theories that people believed because they greatly simplified the model of how markets behave and enabled MPT. The clash between the theoretical models and reality was the basis for in the old popular joke about a University of Chicago economist, famous for his fervor in championing efficient markets, who sees a $20 bill on the street. What, the listener is asked, happens to the money? The answer is "it was never there. If it had existed, the efficient market would have arbitraged it away."

The efficient market hypothesis is certainly a simplifying assumption. In many ways, it is the perfect myth: Easy to understand, powerful in its explanatory power, and wrong.

The World Changes. Markets Evolve.

Institutionalization and Concentration of Assets

When Markowitz examined the capital markets, they featured a far different landscape from what we see today. The markets of the 1950s through the early 1980s were dominated by retail investors, with low levels of institutional investment and little ownership concentration. The asset managers of the time were overwhelmingly active stock and bond pickers; investible passive index funds were not commercially available until 1973. Derivatives existed but were limited; interest rate futures began trading in 1975. Computing power was expensive. The internet was decades away from being a force. Investors still looked at fine print newspaper stock tables for closing stock prices.

This was the status quo and had been for decades. Although market structure was never an explicit assumption for MPT, those were the capital markets Markowitz knew. While the evolution of market structure, including concentration, nationalization, computerization, globalization, and other aspects of today's capital markets have been widely remarked upon, it is striking how little has been analyzed vis-à-vis market structure and MPT.

When Markowitz proposed MPT, institutions owned only 8 percent of the US equity market.[39] Fast forward to the second decade of the twenty-first century when institutional owners and managers (e.g. Government Pension Fund [Japan], Norges Bank, BlackRock, Vanguard, etc.) control about 80 percent of publicly traded equity.[40] This unprecedented concentration is paralleled in most jurisdictions, although the composition of ownership varies. In some emerging markets, family and closely held groups dominate, while large money managers and asset owners tend to dominate in the advanced economies.[41] Within the institutionalization of investing generally is the parallel growth of concentration of ownership among institutional investors. In the UK and the USA, for example, the largest 20 institutional owners hold about 55 percent of all traded equities, which is also historically unprecedented.[42] (It should be noted that, looking through the institutional concentration of asset ownership and management, the ultimate investors are themselves increasingly concentrated. As an example, the wealthiest 10 percent of US households indirectly own or benefit from 84 percent of the US stock market.[43])

That concentration matters. At the time that Markowitz was writing, the market impact of any single investor was negligible and likely to be negated by a different investor. Here is the analogy: If you walk across the room you will have, in some way, affected the gravitational pull of the earth on the moon. But nobody (except perhaps a theoretical astrophysicist) cares, because the impact is so small as to be unobservable, and, in addition, it is likely cancelled out by someone else, somewhere, walking in the opposite direction. Markowitz and Malkiel ignored your investments' impact on the overall market for the same reason. Dispersed market investors are a necessity for the "random walk" hypothesis to "work," because the simplifying assumption of you being a price taker was 99.999 percent correct, and the residual just did not matter enough to care about. But in a concentrated market, a large investor selling or buying can, indeed, affect price, particularly when several act in the same manner. Thus, the rise of "risk on, risk off" markets.

Computers, Complexity, and Tight Coupling

As fast and dramatic as was the institutionalization of capital, another revolution might have changed capital markets even more. Computing power increased a trillion times between 1956 and 2015.[44] A trillion times is difficult to visualize, so here are some examples: The Apollo Guidance Computer that plotted how to let man land on the moon in 1969 had the computing power of two Nintendo game consoles. Storing data in the 1970s meant buying a 16-square-foot IBM device that weighed a ton. It held all of five megabytes.[45] Today you can buy a five-terabyte hard drive for your home computer that weighs about a quarter of a pound for little over $100.[46]

As previously noted, high-frequency trading and other forms of exploitation of information inefficiencies have challenged the random walk theory in ways that its early champions could only have imagined. But computing power affects market structural issues, as well as the assumption of informational efficiency, and these factors further denigrate whatever objective truth that random walk theory might have had.

Famed risk expert Richard Bookstaber, the author of *A Demon of Our Own Design* (2007), emphasizes this point. As he notes, markets are complex systems: "Complexity means that an event can propagate in nonlinear and unanticipated ways." Borrowing a semantic from the field of engineering, he also notes that investment markets feature "tight coupling," wherein one action or process sparks another, with no opportunity for intervention to stop it from progressing.[47] Since Bookstaber's original observations, increased use of innovations such as algorithmic trading, trading bots, new derivatives, exchange-traded products, the trend towards indexed products, and a host of other market developments make market price dynamics even more of a study in complexity.

As Bookstaber states, complexity's key issue for investors are not spikes in volatility or even "the behavior of individual markets, but the concurrent big and unexpected moves among markets. It's the surprising linkages that suddenly appear between markets that should not have much to do with each other and the failed linkages between those that should march in tandem." In other words, markets are not rational, and prices do not manifest as random walk patterns. "Complexity," he explains, "means that an event can propagate in nonlinear and unexpected ways... For financial markets, complexity is spelled d-e-r-i-v-a-t-i-v-e-s."[48]

Bookstaber makes explicit how complexity and tight coupling affect investors trying to practice MPT by being rational and risk-averse. "Investors depend on correlation for hedging and diversifying. And nothing hurts more than to think that you are well hedged and then to discover you are not hedged at all."[49] If, as Warren Buffet said, "derivatives are financial weapons of mass destruction,"[50] then Bookstaber claims that they are aimed directly at the random walk, efficient market, and modern portfolio theories, at least in terms of the ability of an investor to use them in the real world, rather than as a normative hypothetical goal. He titled his article "The Myth of Noncorrelation."[51]

Uncertainty Versus Risk

Why are informational efficiency and efficient markets critical to MPT? They allow the math that defines and calculates an efficient portfolio for a rational investor, based on three capital market assumptions: Expected return, expected risk, and expected correlation. Thus far we have examined challenges to rationality (from Keynes, Simon, Twersky, and Kahneman); to pricing (market concentration resulting in price making, Gilson and Kraakman, lack of information efficiency) and correlations (complexity and tight coupling). But what of volatility?

Remember, volatility itself is a simplifying assumption. It simplifies in two ways. First, as noted earlier, and as will be discussed at length in later chapters, MPT's use of volatility as a risk metric means that it is indifferent to the source of the risk. Leaving aside, for the moment, that ignoring the root cause makes it impossible to mitigate risk and therefore improve the efficiency of a portfolio; it also ignores the fact that some investors have preferences about the nature of risk that they are willing to take, and can tolerate very different volatility bands around the expected price, depending upon the source of the risk. That, of course, is not being rational, but it is a fact. Central banks, for example, dislike credit risk in the bonds that they own, but might accept a certain amount of inflation risk. The second simplification is the assumption that all risks create volatility that can be measured mathematically.

If we drop the assumption of risk as probability expressed in volatility, we enter a far more complex world of what Frank Knight about a hundred years ago called uncertainty (as opposed to probabilistic risk). Uncertainty is not being able to know the probabilities of future events, as well as of what Nassim Taleb called black swan events (tail risk often impossible to usefully calculate) that could not be or were not foreseen.[52] Pretending that there is an efficient market which features calculable, probabilistic volatility around rational expectations of future prices sidesteps the infinite and ultimately unsolvable variable problem inherent in a Knightian/Talebian vision of the world. (As the section on CAPM indicates, it conflates risk and uncertainty.)

Once one admits that investors are not homogenous, but have different access to and interpretations of information (think bounded rationality; heuristics; quantitative model bias; information asymmetry; and prospect theory), then the market cannot reflect fundamental value, either at a moment in time, or over time, nor can it reach some hypothetical equilibrium, or perhaps even a range of equilibria points around which it oscillates. The extreme, but obvious (if only in hindsight) cases of uncertainty manifest themselves in financial bubbles and black swan events, including ones that are generated by the market itself or second-order effects of the market (e.g. mortgage securitization prior to the 2008 financial crisis),[53] as well as those that stem from the non-market events, such as the Covid-19 pandemic of 2020, which saw the S&P 500 tumble 12 percent from its all-time price high to a full-blown correction in just six trading days.[54]

MPT Devours Its Children

Indexation and Super Portfolios

In the Greek myth, Cronus devours his children in a failed attempt to maintain power, but Zeus, Cronos's greatest offspring, defeats him. Today the Titans are viewed as important predecessors to the Olympians, who were themselves later overcome by monotheism.

Index funds − an investment program designed to accept the risk/return of the market without any attempt to beat it − can be considered MPT's Zeus − in that they are, in some ways, MPT's most successful and muscular child. However, they might also be the one that ultimately forces MPT to be similarly recognized as an important and powerful theory, but one that must be surpassed. At some point in the future, it is possible that MPT will be remembered for its important transitional role to a more holistic investment paradigm, rather than as a stable end state.

Index funds have certainly proven muscular. Bill Fouse and John McQuown developed the first successful commercial index fund at Wells Fargo in 1971 as an efficient and low-cost way to invest. Supported by Malkiel's theoretical work (and the efficient market hypothesis generally), Fouse and McQuown argued that few active managers could consistently beat the overall risk/return profile of the market over time. By reducing cost, they argued that the overall return for investors who accepted the market return, minus small fees, would be better than the overall return for investors who hired active managers attempting to outperform the market for products with higher fees. Four years later, Vanguard founder John Bogle popularized index funds for retail investors,[55] and the world of investing has never been the same.[56] As at 2019, index funds accounted for about $8.5 trillion in assets under management (some 39 percent of long-term collective fund products in the USA). That is up from just 18 percent ten years earlier. Indeed, there is now as much invested in indexed products in the US as there were in all collective fund products in 2009.[57]

Jeffrey Wurgler argues that the massive growth of indices and index-linked investing (apparent even when he wrote in 2010) distorts equity prices and traditional risk-return tradeoffs alike. One effect of the growth of index funds has been the phenomenon that Wugler calls "super portfolios," the de facto price co-movements of numbers of stocks and portfolios as they are implicitly linked by similar investment philosophies and (MPT-based) products and techniques, responding to developments in similar ways.[58]

Wurgler calls this the "index inclusion effect." He notes this is only the beginning of the problem, as the inclusion effect is a one-off event, although it can happen many times in a year as new firms are included in, or banished from, for example, the S&P 500. Longer-term and more important, however, are what he calls co-movement and detachment effects. Co-movement refers to what Claessens and Yafeh describe when "…firms' returns experience an increase in comovement with the rest of the index, reflected in higher *beta* and great explanatory power of the market return." In other words, a specific firm can ride an index apart from its actual, underlying fundamental financial and economic profile.[59] There is a certain irony in the fact that index investing, although based on EMH, is typically done by investors who do not even know the names of all the stocks that comprise the index, which is a fundamental negation of EMH's need for investor and market rationality and Malkielian assumptions of information efficiency.

The detachment effect, linked to co-movement, is when an index component drifts away from the market – a price detachment in Wugler's terms which he calculates was in 1997 a 40 percent premium for inclusion in the S&P 500.[60] Others find a lower premium, but a premium nonetheless. The mispricing owing to index inclusion is clearly a complete violation of evaluating portfolio risk in terms of mean-variance volatility, which is a core tenet of MPT.

Over time, the unintended result is that MPT's goal of an efficient portfolio is perverted, as the index fund itself becomes the justification for the index being efficient, which continues the cycle by attracting more capital.[61] In a sense, this turns the efficient market hypothesis on its head, becoming less and less efficient as indexes (and exchange-traded funds) are moved not by information as the efficient market hypothesis holds, but can themselves move markets (the super portfolio effect). We might call this the inefficient portfolio hypothesis.

Almost by definition super portfolios can move markets, as Sullivan and Xiong found: "Such trading commonality then gives way to a rise in systematic fluctuations in overall demand, which, in turn, leads to a fundamental impact on the overall market and investors' portfolios. In short, the growth in trading of passively managed equity indices corresponds to a rise in systematic market risk."[62] This contradicts the core MPT idea that investing is atomistic, stochastic, and random and that systemic risk is strictly external to portfolio behavior.

In sum, MPT provided the intellectual foundation for indexation but never considered the effects of its own widespread adoption, especially in the context of increasingly massive investor concentration. This is a simple logical fallacy – the fallacy of composition that assumes that something that is true for a part of the whole is also true for the whole. MPT could work reasonably well in non-concentrated markets, and when in those markets many or most investors were not using MPT strategies and techniques. Hypothetically, even in low concentrated markets, a tipping point would be reached when large numbers (50 percent? 80 percent?) of investors acted in similar ways on similar information. This is one element of the argument behind random walk hypotheses but, as pointed out previously, assumes each investment actor either ignores or is ignorant of the possible or actual moves of other investors. Empirically this is not and has never been the case. This was Poincaré's point about the nature of human affairs compared, say, with Newtonian physics models. Given that actors are in various way interdependent, randomness does not function, and certainly does not function in a pure, complete way. Given the recent and current massive growth of market concentration, the fallacy of composition is far more potent than in low concentrated markets.

Some of MPT's Real-World Impacts

The growth of index funds has had unintended consequences not just in the financial markets, but in the real world as well. Two separate studies determined that inclusion in prominent investment indices and the concurrent change in ownership of the companies (which is what the cash flows into the index products represents) seriously affect how companies are governed, both structurally and strategically. Index inclusion causes fundamental corporate governance changes such as an increase in the number of independent directors at a company, changed takeover defences, and more equal voting rights. It even changes research and development budgets.[63]

The widespread adoption of diversification, whether through index funds or simply by investors selecting scores, or even hundreds or thousands of securities, together with the institutionalization of capital had impacts not only on the financial markets and on the issuers of those securities, but on at least some of those investors themselves. It caused a number of investors to view themselves not primarily as stock-pickers or even asset allocators seeking to create least-variance portfolios per MPT, but as universal owners (e.g. Norway's Pension Fund Global, Japan's Government Pension Investment Fund).

The universal owner hypothesis (written about extensively by one of this book's authors, James P. Hawley) is to look beyond the capital markets, to the real world.[64] Core to the universal ownership proposition is that broadly diversified large owners and asset managers will, inevitably, internalize a proportion of the (negative and positive) economic externalities each firm in its portfolio creates. In the case of negative externalities, that makes for sub-optimal economic performance, as an externality is by definition a market failure. As Universal Owners (UOs) hold a more or less representative cross section of the whole economy as represented by the markets they have an economic (and broadly a socioeconomic) interest in minimizing and mitigating negative externalities and fostering positive ones. Note that this is an economic argument, not a relative financial one involving financial market-based benchmarks which measure under- or out-performance of a portfolio against some version of a market beta. The implication of UOs for MPT is to link a diversified portfolio's performance not (only or perhaps even) to its mean-variance risk/performance profile, but rather to its impact on and impact from actual non-financial performance of its component firms.

MPT's hermetically sealed math and focus on volatility, rather than the root causes of the risks that create volatility, make it ill-suited for that effort. Which leads us to the MPT Paradox and chapter 2.

Notes

1 Burton Malkiel. *A Random Walk Down Wall Street.* (Ipad 12th edition, pp. 32–33)
2 Harry Markowitz. "Portfolio Selection", *Journal of Finance*, Vol. 7, No. 1. (Mar. 1952), p. 77
3 www.idioms.online/put-all-your-eggs-in-one-basket, accessed September 4, 2020.
4 Michael Useem and David Hess. *Governance and Investments of Public Pensions*, Chapter 7 in "Pensions in the public sector," Olivia S. Mitchell and Edwin C. Hustead, eds, Pension Research Council, The Wharton School, University of Pennsylvania Press (2001), p. 136.
5 *General Investment Policies for the New York State Common Retirement Fund* (August 1, 2017). At: www.osc.state.ny.us/pension/generalpolicies.pdf Accessed November 2, 2019.
6 The divorce of MPT-built portfolios from the actions of companies in the real world gave birth to the modern corporate governance movement. However, until the advent of third-stage corporate governance, as discussed in chapter 5, the discipline of corporate governance was added atop MPT-based investing. Indeed, MPT driven investing was the motivation for a number of the most active corporate governance advocates. The New York City's pension funds and the California Public Employees' Retirement System fund in America, and the BT Pension Scheme in the UK, justified their governance activities by saying that the constructs of MPT, such as indexation and asset allocation, negated their ability to sell if they did not agree with the corporate management of a company whose stock they owned. In effect, the adherence to MPT-based and efficient-market-theory influence investing limited their "exit" option, leaving them with only the option of "voice" to mitigate concerns.
7 See David Pitt-Watson and Hari Mann. "The Purpose of Finance Why Finance Matters: Building an industry that serves its customers and society," 2017, Pensions Insurance Corporation (London); and James Hawley and Jon Lukomnik, "The Purpose of Asset Management," March 2018, Pension Insurance Corporation (London).

8 As we note later, there are myriad systematic risks that now comprise beta or "smart beta." But, initially, beta was a single-factor model related to the volatility of the market in which one invested, as determined by the benchmark, such as the S&P 500.

9 Harry M. Markowitz. "Foundations of Portfolio Theory", Nobel Lecture, December 7, 1990, in *The Founders of Modern Finance: Their Prize-winning Concepts and 1990 Nobel Lectures*, The Research Foundation of the Institute of Chartered Finance Analysts (1991), p. 35.

10 Donald MacKenzie. *An Engine not a Camera: How Financial Markets Shape Markets* (MIT Press, 2006).

11 A similar performative approach to economic theory generally is taken by Daniel Breslau, "Economics invests the economy: Mathematics, statistics and models in the work of Irving Fisher and Wesley Mitchell", *Theory and Society*, June 2003, Vol. 32, Issue 3, pp. 279–411.

12 Andrew W. Lo. *Adaptive Markets: Financial Evolution at the Speed of Thought* (Princeton University Press: 2017), pp. 209–14, specifically on math based "physics envy" beginning most influentially with Paul Samuelson.

13 See, Lo, *op. cit.* pp. 108–110 on the theory of mind.

14 Justin Fox. *The Myth of the Rational Market* (New York: 2009) traces the history of this idea among leading economists in the 20th century, pp. 3–25. (Hyman Minsky, *Stabilizing the Unstable Economy* (1986, New York). See also, Lo, *op. cit.*, pp. 19–20.

15 Milton Friedman. "The methodology of positive economics," in *Essays in Positive Economics* (University of Chicago, 1966, pp. 3–16; 30–46), accessed at: http://kimoon. co.kr/gmi/reading/friedman-1966.pdf. Markowitz himself later in life noted that these assumptions were clearly not true. See Peter L. Bernstein, *Capital Ideas Evolving* (New York: 2007) p. 105.

16 Rational expectation theory is the opposite of Simon's concept of bounded rationality. Although beyond the scope of our discussion, it essentially generalizes and in so doing changes the assumption of each individual acting rationally, while arguing that there is a convergence of markets taking account of various actors' rational expectations. See for example, Stephen M. Sheffrin, *Rational Expectations* (2nd ed., Cambridge, 1996).

17 See Peter Earl. *The Legacy of Herbert Simon in Economic Analysis* (2001: Elgar); and Hugh Schwartz, "Herbert Simon and Behavioral Economics", *The Journal of Socio-Economics* (Vol. 31:2, 2002), pp. 181–89.

18 Burton Malkiel. *A Random Walk Down Wall Street* (Kindle, 12th ed.), for example pp. 178–81 for his discussion of the efficient market hypothesis and market rationality.

19 Thomas J. Sargent. "Rational Expectations" at: www.econlib.org/library/Enc/Ra tionalExpectations.html

20 Burton Malkiel. op. cit. pp. 98–99.

21 Justin Fox. *The Myth of the Rational Market* (New York, 2009), pp. 7–8.

22 This aphorism has been variously attributed to John Maynard Keynes and A. Gary Schilling. https://quoteinvestigator.com/2011/08/09/remain-solvent. Accessed May 9, 2020.

23 Narasimhan Jegadeesh and Sheridan Titman. "Returns to Buying Winners and Selling Losers: Implications for Stock Market Efficiency," *The Journal of Finance*, Vol. 48, No. 1. (March 1993).

24 www.investopedia.com/terms/c/capm.asp. Accessed September 11, 2020.

25 André F. Perold. "The Capital Asset Pricing Model," *Journal of Economics Perspectives*, Vol 18, No. 3 (Summer 2004), p. 13. Risk is defined as incremental risk when part of a portfolio, not the individual 'stand alone' risk of one stock in a portfolio.

26 Burton Malkiel. *op. cit.*, p. 209.

27 www.investopedia.com/terms/c/capm.asp. Accessed September 11, 2020.

28 Bernstein. *op. cit.*, pp. 105; 166. Markowitz found CAPM "a thing of beauty" but noted that its assumptions, like his own, need to be noted when theoretical models are applied to the real world. Ibid., pp. 107; 167.

29 Ibid., p. 168.

30 Harvey, Campbell R. and Liu, Yan. *A Census of the Factor Zoo* (February 25, 2019). Available at SSRN: https://ssrn.com/abstract=3341728 or http://dx.doi.org/10.2139/ssrn.3341728

31 See John H. Cochrane. "Discount Rates," NBER working paper 16972, April 2011, at: https://www.nber.org/papers/w16972 for factor explosion. See also Jennifer Bender, Remy Briand, Dimitris Melas, Raman Aylur Subramanian, "Foundations of Factor Investing," January 1, 2015 at: https://papers.ssrn.com/sol3/papers.cfm?abstract_id=2543990.

32 See Daniel Kahneman and Amos Tversky. "Prospect theory: An analysis of decision under risk," *Econometrica* (47:2), March 1979, pp. 263–92.

33 Ronald J. Gilson and Reinier Kraakman. "The mechanism of market efficiency," *Virginia Law Review*, 70:4, 1984, pp. 549–644.

34 See Lynn A. Stout. "The Mechanisms of Market Inefficiency: An introduction to the new finance," *The Journal of Corporation Law*, 28 (Summer 2003), pp. 635–669. See also, Lo, op. cit., pp. 213–14, where she argues, as have many others, that neoclassical economists and MPT innovators had "physics envy", while they should have had biology envy, the latter concerned with complex, interactive systems, while the former (in it Newtonian and only Newtonian form) was a non-complex system.

35 Burton Malkiel, *op. cit.*, p.179.

36 Ibid. p. 180.

37 See for instance, Chamberlain, Gary and Michael Rothschild. (1983). "Arbitrage, Factor Structure, and Mean-Variance Analysis on Large Asset Markets," *Econometrica*, 51(5); Chen, Nai-Fu, Richard Roll and Stephen A. Ross. 1986. Economic Forces and the Stock Market, *Journal of Business*, 59(3): 383–403; Ross, Stephen. (1976). The arbitrage theory of capital asset pricing, *Journal of Economic Theory*, 13 (3): 341–360.

38 See, for example, Svea Herbst-Bayliss and Lawrence Delevingne. "Hedge fund traders from a legendary desk at Goldman Sachs have lost billions of dollars," Reuters, March 27, 2017.

39 Luis A. Aguilar. Commissioner, Securities and Exchange Commission, Speech to Georgia State University, J. Mack Robinson College of Business, April 19, 2013. www.sec.gov/news/speech/2013-spch041913laahtm.

40 Charles McGrath. "80% of equity market cap held by institutions," *Pensions & Investments*, April 25, 2017, at: www.pionline.com/article/20170425/INTERACTIVE/170429926/80-of-equity-market-cap-held-by-institutions. This institutional ownership is heavily concentrated among the largest asset owners and managers.

41 Al De La Cruz, A. Medina, and Y. Tang. "Owners of the World's Listed Companies," OECD Capital Market Series, Paris (2019).

42 Ibid., p. 24.

43 Patricia Cohen. "We all have a stake in the stock market, right? Guess again", *The New York Times*, February 18, 2018, at: www.nytimes.com/2018/02/08/business/economy/stocks-economy.html. Based on Edward N. Wolf, "Household wealth trends in the united states, 1962 to 2016: Has middle class wealth recovered?", working paper 24085, National Bureau of Economic Research, Washington, DC, November 2017.

44 Nick Routley. "Visualizing the Trillion-Fold Increase in Computing Power," *The Visual Capitalist*, November 4, 2017, at: www.visualcapitalist.com/visualizing-trillion-fold-increase-computing-power.

45 Ibid.

46 Product specifications are for Seagate Backup Plus 5TB USB 3.0/USB 2.0 External Hard Drive

47 See, for example, at http://rick.bookstaber.com/2007/09/myth-of-noncorrelation.html. Accessed May 13, 2020.
48 Ibid.
49 Ibid.
50 Warren Buffet. Chairman's Letter, *Berkshire-Hathaway 2002 annual report.*
51 *Op. cit.*
52 Frank Knight. *Risk. Uncertainty and Profit* (Boston, 1921); Nassim Taleb. *The Black Swan* (New York, 2007); Lo, *op cit.*, pp. 51–56.
53 Lynn A. Stout. *op. cit.*, p. 20, makes a similar point based on a somewhat different argument.
54 William Watts. "S&P 500 tumbles from record finish to correction in just 6 trading days as stock-market rout accelerates," MarketWatch, February 28, 2020, available at: www.marketwatch.com/story/dow-sp-500-enter-correction-territory-as-stock-market-selloff-rolls-on-for-6th-straight-day-2020-02-27. Accessed Mary 25, 2020.
55 Robert E. Litan. "In Defense of Most, But Not All, Financial Innovation", p. 18 available at: www.brookings.edu/wp-content/uploads/2016/06/0217_financial_innovation_litan.pdf. Accessed November 9, 2019.
56 Ibid. p. 17.
57 60th ed. of *Investment Company Fact Book*, Investment Company Institute, 2020.
58 Wurgler, J. 2010. "On the economic consequences of index-linked investing," NBER Working Paper No. 16376. Issued September 2010.
59 Stijn Claessens and Yishay Yafeh. "Additional to market indices and the comovement of stock returns around the world," IMF Working Paper, March 2011, p. 3. See also Hirofumi Suzuki. "Comovement and index fund trading effect: evidence from the Japanese stock market," *Economics Bulletin*, AccessEcon, Vol. 35(2), pp. 949–958. The underlying idea in these studies is the importance of indexing demand.
60 Ibid., p. 8.
61 This should not be understood to mean that there is not concern on the part of some for system health or for various trends in the larger market, social and environmental spheres. For example, the head of the giant $1.4 trillion Japanese Government Pension Investment Fund expressed concern about the growth, size, and impact of passive investing's impact on market efficiency. Hiromichi Mizuno, the fund's head, was concerned that less efficient market signals (owing to incomplete price discovery) would hurt real growth if and when indexation reached a tipping point, arguing that, "We are long term and a universal owner, so we need to make sure that the market will continue to be efficient." To this end, the Fund is increasing active trading compared with passive investing (James Mackintosh, "Streetwise", *The Wall Street Journal* (August 18, 2017, B1).
62 Rodney N. Sullivan and James X. Xiong. "How Index Trading Increases Market Vulnerability," *Financial Analysts Journal*, Vol. 68, No. 2, 2012. pp. 7–84
63 Martijn Cremers, Ankur Pareek, and Zacharias Sautner. "Short-term institutions, analysts recommendation and mispricing," (2017) at: https://papers.ssrn.com/sol3/papers.cfm?abstract_id=2190437&rec=1&srcabs=2285470&alg=1&pos=8; and, Appel, Ian; Cormley, Todd; and Keim, Donald. "Passive Investors, Not Passive Owners,", at: https://papers.ssrn.com/sol3/Papers.cfm?abstract_id=2475150.
64 See James P. Hawley and Andrew T. Williams. *The Rise of Fiduciary Capitalism* (University of Pennsylvania Press, 2000). There is a very large volume of literature on different aspects of universal ownership among academics and practitioners.

2 The MPT Paradox

What is the purpose of investing? That's not a trick question. Nor is it a common one, but it should be. If you do not have a purpose, how to you know if you succeed or fail? As Hall of Fame baseball player Yogi Berra once said, "If you don't know where you're going, you'll end up somewhere else."[1] That's exactly what's happened with investing. We have ended up somewhere else.

That "somewhere else" – the least variance portfolio espoused by MPT as an investor's goal – is a strange place, where the financial markets are somehow viewed as apart from the real world; where the manifestation of risk as volatility is core, but the causes of risk such as climate change or country risk or pandemics are not considered by the math; where success is measured by performance against internal capital market benchmarks like the S&P 500, rather than against real-world needs such as our ability to buy a house or retire in comfort or fund job growth. The result has been a profound alienation between capital markets, the non-financial economy, and the broader economy and society. The financial services industry remains the least trusted industry of any measured by the respected Edelman Trust Barometer – and has been for the past five years running.[2]

Rather than MPT's goal, we suggest that investing has two primary objectives: one for investors and one for society and the economy as a whole.[3] For investors, investing should provide a risk-adjusted return. That is true whether the investor is an individual or a multi-national institution. That might seem familiar, but as we shall see, a truly risk-adjusted return differs materially from an MPT-defined least variance portfolio. For society and the economy, investing is a decentralized, market-driven method to allocate capital. It is Adam Smith's "invisible hand." The financial system, by aggregating savers' capital and putting it to use, can, as the 3rd Lord Rothschild put it, facilitate "the movement of money from point A, where it is, to point B, where it is needed."[4] Lord Rothschild was referring to banking, but with the evolution of the financial system (including capital markets, private equity funds, direct lenders, and other financial institutions), banks no longer have a monopoly on intermediation – the term for the aggregating and reusing of financial capital. Mr. Smith's invisible hand has grown exponentially bigger.[5] Again, this does not seem much different from any traditional MPT theorist's allocation of capital, but it is.

When investors change their methods to consider systemic risks, that also changes the allocation of capital.

We will return to intermediation, but for now, let us focus on the creation of a risk-adjusted return for investors.

Not all investors have the same tolerance for risk. Perhaps more interestingly, not all investors view the same specific causes of financial risk similarly. Various types of investors have particular aversions or affinities to different types of risks, creating a pattern of specific risk avoidance and risk acceptance behaviors. Banks, for instance, are skittish about liquidity risk, as being illiquid at a time when depositors want their money back can cause a "run" on the bank and enterprise-level failure. By contrast, endowments and foundations, as investors with somewhat predictable long-lived liabilities and cash flows, often seek out illiquid investments for the returns that they can generate. Central banks are notoriously averse to credit risk; the possibility that they could lose some of their principle owing to a counterparty's inability or unwillingness to repay. There are almost an unlimited number of causes of risk, as the attached figure from consultancy Capital Market Risk Advisors shows (see Figure 2.1). We particularly note the caveat; this exhausting but not exhaustive galaxy of risks is a partial listing. However, as noted in chapter 1, despite the virtually unlimited, different risk seeking/risk avoidance behaviors of specific investors, MPT distills all those sources of risk to a single impact metric: Volatility. The galaxy of risks, both known and unknown, are irrelevant to MPT. Now, as human beings, we might care for the workers who suffer in stressed economies; for the societal fraying that comes from high levels of income inequality; for the essential

Figure 2.1 Galaxy of Risks
Courtesy of Capital Markets Risk Advisors. Used with permission.

unfairness of gender, racial, ethic, and sexual orientation discrimination; and for the lives lost and ruined in conflict areas. But MPT is bloodless. For MPT, the specific causes of volatility only matter to the extent that they cause price movements to correlate or do not, which would increase/decrease volatility in a portfolio of assets.

From an MPT-blindered point of view, that might make sense, because diversification – MPT's greatest strength – works for idiosyncratic risk, such as that caused by the management of a specific company in executing its strategy. But MPT provides no tools to deal with systematic risks – such as those caused by climate change or a global financial crisis – which affect all securities or a large swath of them. As MPT does not care about the causes of systemic risks and the resultant non-diversifiable systematic impacts on the capital markets, the theory simply does not consider the ability to do anything about them. There is no MPT tool to diversify away from, avoid, or mitigate non-diversifiable systematic risk; the idea of actually dealing with those sources of risk in order to mitigate them is a foreign idea to MPT. However, as we will later see, these systematic risks matter more to investors than do the idiosyncratic risks that define Stock A versus Stock B, or Bond X versus Bond Y.

Indeed, one practical problem with MPT is that its lack of a way for investors to mitigate systematic risks, even while touting the power of diversification, can sometimes encourage promiscuous diversification; that is, investors will rely on diversification in situations when they actually face non-diversifiable systematic risk. This is the investing equivalent of Maslow's hammer theorem: "It is tempting, if the only tool you have is a hammer, to treat everything as if it were a nail."[6] In such cases, diversification might hurt, not help, as the false sense of security that it provides can blind investors and other financial market participants to the building risk. Indeed, it could unwittingly contribute to risk contagion to other investments, thereby increasing the systemic risk to the financial system, which, in turn, creates even more non-diversifiable systematic risk, in a risk-magnifying spiral between the capital markets and the real economy. Increasing reliance on diversification in the face of systematic risk is a bit like continuing to throw a boomerang that not only comes back to hit you, but also increases in size and velocity as it moves along. Together with numerous other factors, this was one of the causes of the 2008–2009 global financial crisis. As one set of observers wrote: "Many loan originators, moreover, were paid based on the number of loans they made, not the quality of those loans. They began writing no- or low-documentation loans... 'liar loans'". They thought that they were protected by the magic of diversification, and they sold most of the loans and kept only small tranches of thousands of them, or hundreds of thousands, what could go wrong?... Diversification turned from a prudent strategy to a justification or sloppy lending... the health of the system depends on someone, somewhere "minding the store."[7]

Simply put, mindless diversification is no substitute for thought.

As the example of the global financial crisis shows, MPT's math is sealed away from the real world and is reliant on a presumption of regularity in terms of markets and market participants doing the right thing.[8] When systemic risks to the environmental, social, or financial systems manifest systematically, the directional price movement of individual securities tends to converge, reducing the value of diversification. Relying on diversification as the primary, or only, risk control in those situations can bring about disaster. That is not necessarily disqualifying, it is just limiting. Trying to apply diversification to systematic risk issues is a recipe for failure. MPT was simply not designed to deal with systematic risks.

That might be more of hindrance than it first appeared to be when Markowitz was writing. Beta – the risk profile of a capital market as determined by the benchmark for that market – turns out to be composed of systematic risk factors with very little idiosyncratic risk left unexplained by them. Yet those uncorrelated idiosyncratic risks are the very ones that diversification can impact.

"Smart" beta, or factor investing, decomposes beta into specific risk exposures, such as style (e.g. value, growth, momentum), size (micro, small, medium, large, and mega capitalization), and other factors (e.g. quality, and more recently, environmental and social governance—ESG) for stocks. Similar factors (such as credit ratings for fixed income, or property type for real estate) occur in other public security markets.

However, MPT's paradigm of being empowered to actively diversify idiosyncratic risk, but told to accept non-diversifiable systematic risk, remains, even when smart beta is considered; just as traditional index investors accept market beta, so to do investors who slice and dice risk factors accept smart beta as it is. They do not take action to try to improve "smart" beta's intellect. MPT simply does not consider that possible in the mathematical bubble in which it exists.

Five Problems With MPT's Alpha/Beta Paradigm

We contend that there are five problems with the alpha/beta paradigm as it is traditionally viewed. The first four are merely huge:

1   Systematic risk, not alpha, drives the vast majority of return.
2   Beta, though a mathematical constant, is anything but constant in the real world.
3   Focusing on alpha results in a misalignment between the asset management industry and the people who entrust their money to it.
4   Alpha and beta are not mutually exclusive. They are a continuum, with many factors which explain risk shifting on that continuum over time to be more "alpha" or more "beta."

But it the fifth problem that is gigantic. We call this the "MPT Paradox," and it gives rise to a fundamental rethink of whether MPT is sufficient to invest wisely going forward. Indeed, it challenges the very idea of what activities constitute investing. Before we delve more deeply into the MPT paradox, let's examine the four predicate issues.

Systematic Risk, Not Alpha, Drives Return

It is not that alpha does not matter to an investor (although investors only want positive alpha, which is impossible on a total market basis), but that the impact of the market return driven by systematic risk swamps virtually any possible scenario created by skillful analysis or trading or portfolio construction. As a number of studies have shown, more than 75 percent of the variability in the return to an investor is caused by systematic risk − that is, some combination of beta and of how much exposure an investor has to that beta. The seminal study is generally considered to be the work by Gary P. Brinson, Randolf Hood, and Gilbert Beerbower[9]. They showed that the selection of asset classes − the choice of how much exposure to stocks, bonds, cash, etc. − explained 93.6 percent of the variability in returns for the pension funds that they were studying. Further academic work, notably by Roger Ibbotson and Paul Kaplan, and by Chris Hensel, Don Ezra, and John Ilkiw, challenged that, suggesting that market movements for a particular time period explained the majority of return variability[10]. While those analyses result in different conclusions about whether it is asset allocation itself or market movements over specific time periods, both sets of studies are consistent in that systematic impacts determine the vast majority of the variability of return. In every study that Ibbotson cites, systematic factors explain 75-94 percent of the variability in return.[11]

Beta, Although a Mathematical Constant, is Anything but Constant in the Real World

Beta is the metric against which you measure the riskiness of your portfolio. Set arbitrarily at the mathematical constant of 1.0, it represents the risk and return of the capital market[12], of which your portfolio is a subset. Each security that you own, and each group of securities (or sub-portfolios, or asset classes, etc.) has a beta. With the beta of the market, as proxied by a benchmark such as the S&P 500 or MSCI All Country World Index (ACWI), deemed to be at 1.0, a "risky" or volatile portfolio would have a beta greater than 1, while a less risky portfolio would have a beta of less than 1. A portfolio that moves in the opposite direction of the market (so the price lowers when the market rises, or vice-versa) would be said to have a negative beta. Here's the problem. The beta of the market might be set at a constant 1.0, but what that 1.0 represents in real-world returns varies both across subsets of the capital markets and over time. Is a high beta portfolio or a low beta portfolio better? For instance, the S&P 500 returned 31.5 percent in 2019, but lost 4.4 percent in 2018[13]. So, in 2019 you wanted a high beta portfolio (it would return more than the market), whereas in 2018 you wanted a low beta portfolio (to lose less than the market), or better yet, a negative beta portfolio. In other words, the beta of market is an internal measurement that tells you nothing about what your returns will be, or were, in the real world. It does not even tell you what relationship you want your specific portfolio to have to the market.

Focusing on Alpha Results in a Misalignment Between the Asset Management Industry and People Who Entrust Their Money to It

Alpha does measure a portfolio manager's skill in selecting how well he/she selects securities and constructs a portfolio against the against the overall risk/ return of the universe of securities from which he/she can select a portfolio. But the purpose of investing is not contained within a universe whose bounds are defined by a trading terminal. The real-world purpose is to build or preserve wealth, or offset a liability, through the creation of a risk-adjusted return. MPT's math, focused as it is on relative return and benchmarking, simply does not deal with this. Consider an average investor saving for retirement or a house or a vacation. Assume that the investor puts $100 into a large cap US equity account during a period when the S&P 500 drops by 10 percent, but his portfolio manager is down by only 8 percent. In the jargon of the business, the portfolio manager has outperformed, with an excess return of 200 basis points. He or she is a hero and likely to receive a very nice bonus. Keep it up, and he or she will soon grace the same business magazine covers and television shows (and now podcasts and social media feeds) that once featured Peter Lynch and Bill Miller. They have outperformed their benchmark, and that will make them a star. But whose goal is that? The asset managers' or the investors'? The investors who entrusted the portfolio manager with their hard-earned money still only have 92 cents on the dollar and are farther away than ever from being able to retire, buy a house, or take a vacation. Returning to first principles reminds us that the purpose of asset management is to create an optimal, or at least acceptable, risk/return profile for his/her investments vis-à-vis the investor's real-world needs. That means total risk/return, not an "alpha-adjusted relative to benchmark risk/return."

The focus on alpha, relative return, and the benchmarks that have become investing's north stars are false proxies for investing's original purpose of effective asset management along the efficient frontier which measures risk against return. Absolute efficiency has become subsumed to benchmark-adjusted efficiency disconnected from the non-financial "real" economy or an investor's real-world needs and desires. Even the semantics used reinforce this erroneous focus on relative return. How far your return deviates from the benchmark is measured by tracking "error," as if the benchmark (at 1.0 beta) somehow always represents a normative level of return desired and deviation from it is therefore problematic. If the goal is to provide risk-adjusted returns, does it make sense to focus on the part of return that only accounts for small minority of that risk/return profile? Focusing on alpha is self-referential. It divorces investing from its purpose.

Alpha and Beta are not Mutually Exclusive

MPT practice considers alpha and beta as distinct and mutually exclusive, defining alpha as "a factor that represents the performance that diverges from a portfolio's beta."[14] Even the math that calculates alpha (the formula is α = return − [risk free rate + (market return − risk free rate) β] relies on that distinction: Academically, alpha is the residual performance that cannot be explained by systematic risk factors.[15] However, as computing power has exploded, analysts have consistently moved returns caused by what were previously considered idiosyncratic factors into categories such as "smart beta" or "factors" or "exposures." In other words, we now explain even more of a specific portfolio's return as caused by systematic risk exposures than when Brinson or Ibbotson studied returns. The result is that dividing total return into alpha and beta is more nuanced and complex today, because what constitutes beta is more nuanced and complex today. And that leaves little pure "alpha" available to investors. These and other developments contribute to what we might call the post-MPT era.

The morphing of the once rock-hard divide between alpha and beta into a semi-permeable-membrane through which alpha and beta spill into each other happens over time and continues to evolve. This is one important element of the post-MPT era. (Others include ESG and its many constituent elements, together with systemic risk awareness.) Half a century ago, a stock picker could have selected a portfolio of small cap growth stocks during a time period when they outperformed and plausibly called his/her outperformance "alpha." He or she would have been lauded for their stock-picking skill. The small cap effect and the impact of growth/value styles were not well appreciated. The portfolio would have been seen as constructed of a series of idiosyncratic risks, rather than a group of stacked trades with similar risks. Today, virtually all the performance differential of such a portfolio against a broad market index would be explained by systematic risk factors. Faced with a portfolio of small capitalization growth stocks, any experienced observer would select a more appropriate benchmark for "the market:" one that fits the risk exposures of that specific portfolio. "Alpha" would probably approach zero (or go negative), with all the performance attributed to various factors also contained in the benchmark. Indeed, today you can buy passive index funds of such a portfolio. This is not a fanciful construct. Warren Buffett is widely considered one of the best investors of the post-MPT era. Yet decomposing his investments into factors finds that he has consistently been overweighting quality, size, value, and low volatility factors, and underweighting growth and dividend yield factors. A theoretical "factor-mimicking" portfolio nearly reproduces Buffett's returns between 1991 and 2017 and shows very little alpha.[16] That is not to criticize Buffett's investing skills, but to say that alpha is largely irrelevant and what is often considered alpha really is not. As the author of the study notes, Buffett "has demonstrated unprecedented skill in selecting factors, constructing a multi-factor portfolio, and adapting the factor mix over time." In the end, Buffett understands that the job is to produce total returns, not alpha returns or factor returns. Just returns. He did so by choosing securities with the correct mix of smart beta exposures.

Hedge funds provide another example of factors that were previously considered contributing to alpha morphing into beta. In the early days of hedge funds, they took advantage of what had been persistent pricing anomalies. A London School of Economics professor studied 40 such anomalies that hedge funds had routinely used to create "alpha." He found that those anomalies are arbitraged away over time.[17] One key variable is how widespread the knowledge of the anomaly is to the marketplace. In this case, he found publication of the anomaly in an academic journal (which accelerated market awareness) materially affected the amount of capital deployed to arbitrage the anomaly.[18]

Examples abound of risk exposures that were previously viewed as idiosyncratic sources of alpha, but are now consisted systematic, such as the increasing research into ESG factors as sources of alpha or smart beta, or both. Various uses of ESG factors, from best-in-class tilts to short-term ESG momentum portfolios that focus on improvement in ESG ratings, have outperformed some traditional benchmarks in the past decade or so.[19] One review of approximately 2,200 studies of corporate performance found that 63 percent of them associated better ESG performance with higher value creation (only 8 percent had negative findings).[20]

More recently, studies have sought to understand the real-world transmission mechanisms that might enable better ESG performance to drive financial performance in corporations, rather than in the financial marketplace. A key study suggests five ways that high-performing ESG companies create value disproportionate to their peers: "ESG links to cash flow in five important ways: (1) facilitating top-line growth, (2) reducing costs, (3) minimizing regulatory and legal interventions, (4) increasing employee productivity, and (5) optimizing investment and capital expenditures."[21] In a different study, Withold Henisz, a Wharton Professor of Management, who co-authored that first study, and co-author James McGlinch found that ESG performance correlates with material events and credit risk, as measured by bankruptcies and credit spreads, which has major implications for credit markets and bond investors.[22] A different, earlier set of researchers found that the cost of capital — whether debt or equity — is lower for firms with strong E and/or S and/or G factors.[23] Recent additional studies have found a variety of transmission phenomena between E and S and/or G performance and corporate financial performance. For example, two scholars examined firms' resilience in the face of the Covid-19 pandemic finding that stocks with higher sustainability ratings fared less worse than a benchmark group, focusing on investor trust.[24] Another study by Serafeim and Yoon found that, "Prices react only to financially material news and the reaction is larger for news that are positive, receive more attention, and social capital related. Firm-specific ESG performance score predicts future news related to social and natural capital issues…This suggests that investors incorporate future expectations about ESG news in ESG performance scores."[25] Two scholars from the University of Sienna and one from Oxford University, working as a team, examining equity prices during the early stages of the Covid-19 pandemic found that price performance was correlated with what they call the materiality intensity; those firms with high ESG ratings and higher materiality intensity performed better (less worse) during this period.[26] Of course, such finds examining data for only a matter of months are not proof, but are strongly indicative, given the massive shifts resulting from Covid-19 dislocations. This is especially so, as other studies by scholars from the University of California, Berkeley, the University of Zurich, and from Harvard working with academics working with State Street Associates, have found similar results. All use different methods.[27]

To the degree that the real-world benefit of such ESG-associated advantages enables such firms to outperform the firms that do not consider ESG factors but are included in the benchmarks for which the higher-performing ESG firms are components, an ESG "alpha" can be embedded in the securities of those corporations. However, that assumes that, like the markets of half a century ago when most did not recognize the systematic nature of small capitalization or growth factors, enough of today's market participants do not widely recognize those ESG advantages. In other words, the assumption of information efficiency that contributes to the efficient market hypothesis is deeply flawed. That is exactly the implication of some of the studies that Friede looked at to determine whether there was ESG alpha. Those researchers found that "Less than a quarter of investment professionals consider extra-financial information frequently in their investment decisions (EY 2015) and just about 10% of global professionals receive formal training on how to consider ESG criteria in investment analysis (CFA Institute 2015)."[28] The implication of those statistics is that most of the market is not (or was not at the time) sophisticated in examining ESG factors; such lack of recognition enabled those factors to be "found" by early movers. Exactly in such alpha seeking is a key indication that alpha and beta might not be as distinct as traditionally assumed. As with the study of the anomalies used by hedge funds, it appears that while ESG factors (or capitalization size, or style, or earnings quality, or myriad other factors now routinely considered systematic) can provide a source of "alpha" for early adopters, over time they become the systematic factors that determine the "beta" of the market as alpha over time reverts to the mean once significantly recognized. As with fitting a growth portfolio to a growth benchmark rather than the S&P 500, or a high-yield bond portfolio to a high-yield benchmark rather than an investment grade bond benchmark, comparing the returns of a portfolio of securities selected for ESG performance to a benchmark which includes systematic ESG factors would probably reduce the available alpha. In other words, to the degree that over time ESG or any other factor is recognized by the larger market, the potential for "alpha" fades, and those systematic factors become smart beta and then part of just plain market beta. The math behind that evolution is somewhat tautological, in that beta is measured against a benchmark. So, for example, comparing a low-carbon portfolio against a standard benchmark such as the MSCI ACWI, as was done pre-2014, means that there would be a mismatch in risk factor exposures. Therefore, the performance variance caused by the low-carbon nature of the portfolio compared with the standard index would be a "residual" not explained by the beta of the benchmark, and the portfolio manager could claim it as "alpha." However, MSCI began publishing a low carbon target version of the ACWI in 2014, and the available alpha to that portfolio would have been diminished, as the MSCI ACWI Low Carbon Target index itself includes the impact of the lower carbon emissions in the portfolio and, therefore, in its arbitrary beta of 1.0.

Therefore, rather than think of alpha and beta as separate and distinct, we view each factor that contributes to market return on a continuum between pure alpha and pure beta, with its position on that continuum dynamic over time, as more or less of the market capital recognizes it as systematic or idiosyncratic and trades it as such. This is both empirically and logically verified, in that alpha does not disappear at a moment in time, but rather decays at various rates, not necessarily linearly. Mature, well-known factors such as style (value/growth), credit quality, and size are more towards the beta end of the continuum. ESG factors, more newly discovered and with data not yet standardized, are closer to the alpha side. Moreover, we note that the increase in computing power available today seems to be driving more and more factors to be discovered and, therefore, regarded as systematic. Academics have now identified at least 382 systematic risk factors, and although other academics (and we) have serious concerns about the validity of some, certainly many are, in fact, robust.[29] In 2018 Morningstar reported almost 1,500 smart beta products traded on exchanges (that does not count separate accounts, which are bespoke for larger investors). Nearly 10 percent of those products were created in 2018 alone.[30] We expect the current explosion in big data analysis and artificial intelligence abilities to continue that trend and that the assets under management in smart beta passive products will grow materially. That should result in some of (what is now considered) alpha being arbitraged away, consistent with the findings of the hedge fund anomaly study. [NB: *While we consider all factors as somewhere on the continuum between alpha (idiosyncratic) and beta (systematic) we will continue to use the terms "alpha" and "beta" as in common usage, in discussing MPT and investing unless otherwise noted.]*

One question worth considering is that if alpha can become beta, can the reverse happen? With the complexity created by hundreds of systematic risk factors being discovered, combined with the increased ease to invest in them thanks to exchange-traded funds (ETF), derivatives, customized benchmarks, and other capital market innovations, as well as computerization, it seems inevitable that asset flows will chase systematic factors associated with recent positive performance, creating a risk on/risk off rotation among those factors. So, could betas become alphas during some time periods? Call this a "specific-risk-factor-on/specific-risk-factor-off" phenomenon. As the analysis of Warren Buffett's investments above shows, such risk factor investing can be very effective, although the excess return would not technically be "alpha," as it would explained by systematic risk factors, rather than idiosyncratic risks (or, in a mathematics sense, a residual value). In 2015 Ron O'Hanley, CEO of State Street Global Advisors observed, "I think the new active, as I would describe it, is in asset allocation. As more and more investors are using these highly developed investment building blocks, they need to put them together in an asset allocation model."[31]

In summary, the math that measures alpha is dependent upon being able to distinguish it from beta, or systematic risk/return. But dividing alpha from beta is a dynamic process, changing as the markets and analytical tools change. First, the amount of residual performance not attributable to beta or "smart beta" is shrinking as computing power grows, and smart beta redefines what is systematic as those factors are communicated to the market. Whether or not small cap growth stocks were a source of alpha in 1952, because the systematic factors were not yet identified and, therefore, they were just as systematic back them and should have been called smart beta is a philosophical and semantic question, not an investing one. Second, we strongly believe that whatever the semantics and philosophy, alpha and beta are on a continuum, with any specific factor able to shift its position relative to being considered as contributing to alpha or beta as less or more capital is deployed to it. In other words, feedback loops encompassing information efficiency, capital allocation decisions, and market dynamics can cause the same factors to be considered alpha or smart beta at different times. Moreover, as O'Hanley suggested, the division between active and passive investing is similarly dynamic, with some viewing the selection of smart betas into a portfolio as the "new active." In effect, he is suggesting that alpha can be sourced from systematic risk factors, a wonderfully if unintentionally ironic revamp of MPT's traditional divorce of alpha from beta. Finally, as alpha is a residual, and beta is measured against a proxy for market opportunity as determined by a benchmark, the beta of a portfolio will approach 1 (the risk of the market), and alpha will approach 0, as the benchmark chosen has more explanatory power.

The rise of systematic factor/smart beta investing and the associated ETFs and other index products based on them also raise interesting and parallel questions for price discovery. Traditionally, researchers viewed price discovery as the province of active, fundamental managers. Indexation, as it was historically capitalization-weighted, reflecting prices that were already market prices, was not thought to contribute to price discovery. For example, Amar Bhide writes that indexation "undermines the pluralism of opinions that help align prices and values."[32] To the extent that indexation affects prices, it is thought to create pricing anomalies, such as Wurgler's superportfolios (discussed in chapter one). But the indexes that dominated the markets that Wurgler and Bhide studied were traditional, capitalization-weighted passive investment vehicles. But if we accept O'Hanley's view that mixing and matching smart betas is the new active, and if we remember that there are 382 factors and some 1,500 smart beta products, the old idea of only active managers contributing to price discovery could be simplistic. Instead, price discovery – which ultimate depends on capital flows into a specific security – becomes a complex matrix of flows. Active managers, making fundamental judgements about that security surely contribute. Traditional capitalization-weighted index funds will affect them as well. But so will factor-based index funds. If, for instance, market participants put money into large cap index funds and into tech index funds, then money will flow into Microsoft, Apple, etc. Should investors choose to invest in biotech indices, money will flow to those securities. If small cap value is in vogue, a different set of companies will benefit. And given the different factors that the index funds try to replicate – size, quality, dividend yield, sector, style, domicile, etc. – the capital flowing into each individual security will be driven by a very pluralistic view of which factors are seeing net inflows or outflows. Think of the price discovery of any individual security as a Venn diagram, with active managers, traditional index funds, and factor-based index funds all overlapping.

The MPT Paradox

As intriguing and impactful as those first four issues are, the MPT paradox lies at the heart of MPT's limited ability to create a desirable risk/return for investors. Simply put, MPT forces investors to focus on that which matters least.

According to MPT, your investments are affected by the market but are unable to affect it. This one-way-valve view of investing creates a plethora of problems and inefficiencies. And it is just plain wrong.

Here's the first issue: If the market rate of return is exogenous to your portfolio, then it makes sense to focus on that which you can control, which is alpha. But, as noted previously, the total market return owing to beta swamps any available return attributable to alpha. Hence the focus on what matters least.

Second, given the interplay between alpha and beta noted above, what does the increasing ability to parse total returns into beta and smart beta mean for diversification, which is the central means of risk control in MPT? As diversification is designed to mitigate idiosyncratic risk, when more and more of the return is explicably due to systematic factors, does that challenge MPT's power by reducing the idea of diversification's salutary impact? How much risk/return of a diversified portfolio is truly idiosyncratic? Or should we be focused on diversifying different systematic factors and add a time dimension, as O'Hanley suggests?

That raises the key corollary question for investors. And it is outside the ability of MPT to illuminate: If we are discovering that more and more risks are systematic, are there ways that investors can ameliorate non-diversifiable risk? Perhaps some type of mitigation is possible, despite MPT's assumption that the causes of volatility are irrelevant, and that market risk is exogenous? In other words, can we affect beta, or, to put it another way, if the entire market were a portfolio, can we affect the risk/return of it, not relative to anything else, but absolutely? Another way to think about this is: Can investors cause the entire market to re-rate, in order to improve the Sharpe ratio of the overall market? (The Sharpe Ratio, named after Nobel Laureate William Sharpe, is the total return of the market, minus the return available from the risk-free rate, divided by volatility.)

As we noted in chapter one, market risk is not exogenous to investing. But those impacts (index affects, super portfolios, as well as risk on/risk off markets caused by capital flows) are unintentional. They are the result of the confluence of the institutionalization of the marketplace and the dominance of MPT. The more consequential question is: "Can investors deliberately impact systematic risk so as to increase return and/or dampen risk?"

In a word: Yes. Investors can build a "better beta," − that is, create a market with a better risk/return (higher Sharpe ratio). Indeed, in some empirical studies there is not a risk/return trade off but rather in the ESG case, lower risk *and* higher return, creating a risk-return trade-on, not a trade-off.[33] That makes sense. As Markowitz said, investors should seek predictability. The difference here is that investors cause the predictability; therefore they can benefit from being positioned in a set of securities before and during the process of the market rerating those securities as lower risk and therefore more desirable.

This is the third − and perhaps most important − negative consequence of the MPT paradox: The assumption of the exogeneity of the total market's risk and return profile and the focus on diversification as the preferred means of risk control, as well as the attention to alpha and relative return, mean that MPT at best ignores − and at worst discourages − efforts to mitigate systematic risk. That is investing malpractice writ large.

MPT traditionalists limit the art of investing (in public securities, at least) to the activity set that is relevant to alpha seeking or beta matching: Security analysis, factor analysis, trading, and portfolio construction. Using non-trading-related tools such as stewardship or disclosure standard-setting to mitigate causes of non-diversifiable systematic risk such as climate change have been dismissed as "political" or "social investing" (see below). There is an internal logic to that dismissal, but that logic is a tautology. If you accept MPT's premise that the causes of beta are exogenous, then you focus on security selection and portfolio construction, so you do not explore your ability to mitigate systematic risk through non-trading methods, so they continue to appear exogenous; which puts the focus back on security selection and portfolio construction, which... As previously noted, while passive and smart beta strategies do not seek alpha, neither do they try to affect beta or the specific risk exposures that they seek or try to avoid. *De facto*, they accept MPT's assertion of beta exogeneity.

The beta exogeneity tautology blinkers our vision, limiting our view to the electronic dots on trading screens and preventing a clear view of the feedback loops between volatility and return in the capital markets and their real world causes. This is yet another paradox: Focusing on diversification as the only tool to minimize volatility does nothing to actually reduce the causes of market-wide volatility, and, as we saw in the global financial crisis example, there can be serious side effects which actually exacerbate volatility. We note that factor investing looks to a host of possible risk elements, not just volatility. Nonetheless, we include it in the MPT tradition, however far it has traveled from Markowitz's original formulation, is that it restricts itself to market-based risk factors (rather than their sources in the real world). Therefore, it does do not escape the MPT paradox, although it might well push the paradox's boundaries.

Of course, if you break any of those circular arguments, the entire tautology breaks down. Fortunately, practice has led theory, a hallmark of the post-MPT era. Various investors have rejected the hermetically sealed math of MPT and focused on the real world in their attempts to mitigate systematic risks. Notice the "s" at the end of risks in the previous sentence. While MPT might disregard the sources of risk and care only about their manifestation as volatility, these investors understand that if you are going to reduce volatility by mitigating the systemic risks that contribute to volatility, then the root causes of the risk matter. Breaking the beta exogeneity tautology means breaking out of the traditional definitions of investing and looking at the real world beyond the trading screen. It often does not involve trading or security selection, but actions like coalition building, affecting public policy, and stewardship. Those activities can have more impact on improving risk/return than even the starriest of star portfolio managers.

We call this type of investor activity "beta activism" because it is designed to affect systematic risk across the entire market, not just at a specific company or a specific security. As we will see in chapter five, this is the distinguishing factor of third stage corporate governance and distinguishes it from the alpha-focused activism of high-profile activists such as Carl Icahn or The Children's Investment Fund. What alpha- and beta-activists have in common is they seek to impact the real world in ways that MPT's walled-off math never contemplated. They take action beyond the electronic blips of their trading screens. However, the differences between alpha- and beta-activists are also stark. Alpha-seeking activists seek to influence the strategy and tactics of a single company, for instance by affecting the choice of a company's CEO, a merger or divestiture, or a company's capital allocation. By focusing on a single company, in which the activist usually holds a material investment, the alpha activist seeks excess return from an idiosyncratic situation. In MPT theory terms, what an alpha activist attempts to do is to improve the risk/return profile of a corporate security by acting to change the risk/return of the corporation (sometimes successfully, sometimes not). This fits neatly into the MPT framework for alpha seeking, except that the successful alpha activist causes the information flow from real-world activity to market price, rather than waiting for market price movement.

By contrast, beta activists target issues and seek to affect systematic risks, rather than target companies, although issue targeting might sometimes take the form of targeting a group of companies that contribute most to systemic risk, e.g. the top 100 greenhouse gas emitting companies in order to combat the systematic market risk from climate change. Beta activists seek root causes of risk, rather than corporate financial underperformers.

In theory, the sum of all the investors' expectations about any systematic risk (e.g. climate change, lack of gender diversity, etc.) is built into the perceived riskiness of "the market." Therefore, if a beta activist can cause a reduction in the perceived riskiness of a systematic risk, the entire market re-rates. That is similar to what happens when the market re-rates a single security targeted by an alpha activist. However, because a systematic risk factor targeted by a beta activist impacts the entire marketplace, even a small systematic risk re-rating can have hundreds of billions of dollars of impact.

Chapter five spotlights six beta activist campaigns. For now, however, let us examine a short case study of one beta activism campaign to understand what is meant by creating "better beta" − that is, changing the total market risk/return − through other-than-trading investment activities.

A $132 Billion Beta Boost

Virtually everywhere around the world, companies are governed by Boards of Directors. While the form and some details (unitary or dual board, how independent from management, whether there is a controlling shareowner, employee representatives etc.) might vary, the basic role of the Board remains the same: To steward the company. How well the Board stewards the company matters. Who is on the Board matters. To whom the Directors feel accountable matters. That is why alpha activist investors often seek board seats. But to a beta activist investor, the goal is not to improve the Board at a specific company, but to improve how every company selects its Board members in order to improve accountability. Beta activists seek to impact broad swathes of the market.

That was the thinking when New York City Comptroller Scott Stringer announced his "Boardroom Accountability Project" (BAP) in November 2014. The Comptroller serves as the investment advisor for the five major New York City defined benefit pension funds, which, at the time, had aggregate assets of some $160 billion.[34] Stringer and the pension fund trustees were frustrated by the inability of shareowners to directly nominate corporate Board members. The United States Securities and Exchange Commission had tried to allow such direct nominations through a process called "proxy access" in 2010, but a lawsuit overturned the SEC rule. There was one exception to that prohibition, however: Shareowners of each individual company could, if they so wished, adopt proxy access through a vote at that company's annual general meeting.[35] However, making that change on a company-by-company basis was expensive and cumbersome. As a result, nobody tried to use that company-by-company strategy until the NYC funds did. At the time of the launch of the Boardroom Accountability Project, only six American companies featured a proxy access rule.

That all changed, however, following Stringer's announcement that the NYC Funds were heading a coalition of large investors attempting to establish proxy access as a new market standard by filing resolutions to mandate proxy access through private ordering. Those institutional investors had the resources to take on − and overcome − the hurdles. They also had the motivation; most of them were universal owners who understood that their returns were linked more to the overall market and to the economy than to their stock-picking or portfolio construction abilities, as good as they were. The specific process that Stringer outlined might have been company-by-company, but the overall campaign certainly was not. They announced the first 75 corporations at which they would fight for proxy access and made it clear that this was about establishing a new market norm. Interestingly, those companies were chosen largely because they were exposed to various other known risks: 33 were in carbon-intensive industries, and 24 had little or no gender, racial, or ethnic diversity on the board. Twenty-five of the companies had problems.[36]

The unusual circumstances around the SEC adopting a rule, then a court staying the rule, then an exception being used to try to implement the rule across a material subset of the marketplace and the surprise announcement by Comptroller Stringer created a natural experiment. As three researchers found, Stringer's announcement caused those 75 companies to experience a 53-basis-point excess return. They noted that Stringer's announcement did not guarantee that proxy access would be adopted, only that it would be proposed at 75 companies. The researchers suggested that market-wide regulation/adoption would probably have resulted in an even larger re-rating across the entire marketplace.[37]

Stringer and the New York City's funds' efforts to be beta activists have largely worked. Proxy access has become something of a de facto market standard, at least among large capitalization US public companies. As at July 2019, less than five years after Stringer's 2014 BAP announcement, more than 600 US public companies featured proxy access rules (up from six), and the number was climbing.[38]

The City funds have since instituted a Boardroom Accountability Project 2.0, announced in 2017, focused on the transparency of how corporations choose their Directors, as well as on the skills, experiences, and diversity of the Board. Approximately two years later, 62 of the targeted companies had added 77 diverse directors to their boards.[39] Again, the focus is on a systematic risk – a lack of diversity – rather than a specific company's situation.

The BAP hints at the magnitude of impact that beta activism can have. It has created a de facto standard for proxy access among large capitalization US public companies. It has (together with many other initiatives) increased diversity among the directors who oversee and guide US public companies. And it has proven the power of beta activism in improving the risk/return of the overall market. At the time of Stringer's announcement, the City's funds held $5.023 billion in the stock of those 75 companies.[40] Based on the 53 basis points of excess return, that means that the BAP created some $266 million in excess return for the City's pension funds. As the City's funds generally hold 1 percent or less of a company's stock, that means that the total market impact was more than $25 billion. The actual impact on total market value over time, as 600 companies have adopted proxy access, is likely to be several times that level. Finally, while the study that examined the BAP noted that the results would probably have been greater, had a proxy access standard been market-wide and set by regulation, even just using the 53 basis points of excess return as the basis, extending the attempt to install proxy access across every listed company at the time of Stringer's announcement would have resulted in an increased market value of some $132.5 billion.[41]

So why has this type of beta activism not been recognized for what it is: An extension of investment risk management to the real-world root causes of systemic risk that create volatility, and therefore, an attempt to mitigate non-diversifiable systematic risk in a way that MPT never contemplated?

We contend there are two reasons:

- The techniques used to create better beta extend far beyond trading and portfolio construction. Many people, including investors, but also regulators, commentators and academics, indoctrinated over the past half century when MPT was ascendant, do not consider these tasks "investing." Jon Lukomnik, one of the authors of this book, was at a private meeting in Washington DC when a regulator asked him how to get more investors involved in serving on various financial regulatory advisory boards. Lukomnik suggested several high-profile institutional investors with corporate governance and corporate stewardship experience whom he thought would be interested, including some involved in the Boardroom Accountability Project. The regulator demurred. "We need *real* investors," he said. He meant people who trade.

- To be a material systematic risk, the root causes tend to be big. As a result, they are usually dramatic and newsworthy (e.g. apartheid in South Africa, climate change, gender diversity). Therefore, when investors tackle those issues, they are often viewed as a series of one-off social or political efforts, rather than sequential manifestations of attempts to build better beta. In some ways, this argument overlaps with the question of intermediation. When investors attempt to mitigate systemic issues such as climate change, some do so by divesting from the securities of certain industries. Those who view the world of investing only through a MPT market price lens and a trading screen accuse beta activists of following a political agenda, rather than maximizing value critics claim that beta activist investors are using social or political lenses to allocate capital. This argument misses two key points. First, not all beta activism relies on investment or disinvestment (exclusions). Many use other tools, as shown by the New York City example and by many others profiled in chapter five. Second, even when capital is being directed or withheld, the criticism ignores the fact that beta activists are part of the market as well, making an informed choice about which risks to accept, much the same way that central banks will not generally take credit risk. Ironically, then, these market purists are suggesting that differences of opinion as to the value of these securities (both societal and financial), which is what creates markets and price discovery, are somehow antithetical to markets. For example, NYC Comptroller Stringer's efforts to install proxy access as a market-wide reform, spotlighted above, were criticized as a politicization of the investing process by the American Council for Capital Formation (ACCF), a pro-corporate management group founded by the former executive vice president of the American Banking Association. The ACCF drew what we consider to be a false dichotomy, arguing that systemic reforms are *ipso facto* unrelated to investing and therefore illegitimate: "… [H]is management of the $190 billion pension funds continues to focus more on shareholder resolutions and social engagement efforts with very little public focus on improving returns."[42] ACCF never seemed to consider the idea that Stringer could be trying to both improve social conditions and returns at the same time. Or that improving social conditions is necessary to improve the pension funds' returns by improving the total market risk/return profile. The relation between the two were dramatically exemplified shortly thereafter, when the Covid-19 pandemic revealed the deep social crevices in, for example, medical care and access and the intertwining of the social and economic systems in supply chain dynamics as well as the demand collapse necessitated by anti-pandemic social distancing and stay-in-place orders.

For critics of beta activism, the fact that these actions attempt to deal with the social, environmental, and financial causes of non-diversified systemic risk means that they are automatically misguided diversions from traditional MPT investment activities.[43] They do not see any link between them and the risk/return profile of the investments. For investors who understand that systematic factors largely determine returns, those actions provide mitigation of systematic risk in a way that MPT never considered and so are core to effective investing in today's world.

Notes

1 www.goodreads.com/quotes/23616-if-you-don-t-know-where-you-are-going-you-ll-end. Accessed August 9, 2019.
2 www.edelman.com/sites/g/files/aatuss191/files/2019-04/2019_Edelman_Trust_Barometer_Financial_Services_Report_1.pdf. Accessed February 10, 2020.
3 James Hawley and Jon Lukomnik. "The Purpose of Asset Management," Pension Insurance Corporation, (London: March. 2018), p. 12.
4 Victor Rothschild, cited in Niall Ferguson. *The Ascent of Money*. (Penguin Press, 2008), p. 65.
5 For example, financial intermediation now accounts for from about two-and-a-half to four times the annual GDP of Germany, France, the USA and the UK. Guillaume Bazot, "The Purpose of Finance: Has efficiency improved in the European finance industry?", Pension Insurance Corporate, October 2018.
6 Abraham H. Maslow. *The Psychology of Science: A Reconnaissance*, HarperCollins (1966).
7 Stephen Davis, Jon Lukomnik, and David Pitt-Watson. *What They Do With Your Money: How the Financial System Fails Us and How to Fix It*, Yale University Press, 2016, pp. 47–48.
8 The divorce of MPT-built portfolios from the actions of companies in the real world was remarked upon by some observers and gave birth to the modern corporate governance movement. But the discipline of corporate governance was added atop MPT-based investing. Indeed, MPT-driven investing was the motivation for a number of the most active early corporate governance advocates. New York City's pension funds and the California Public Employees' Retirement System in the USA and the BT Pension Scheme in the UK justified their governance activities by saying that the constructs of investing, such as indexation and asset allocation, negated their ability to sell if they did not agree with the corporate management of a company whose stock they owned. In effect, the adherence to MPT-based investing limited their "exit" option, leaving them with only the option of "voice" to mitigate concerns. See Jon Lukomnik, "Why We Bother: A Primer in How Activism Enhances Returns", 2 Fordham J. Corp. & Fin. L. 5 (1997). Available at: https://ir.lawnet.fordham.edu/jcfl/vol2/iss1/1.

9 Gary P. Brinson, Randolf Hood, and Gilbert Beerbower. "Determinants of Portfolio Performance," *Financial Analysts Journal*, Vol. 42, No. 4, July/August 1986, pp. 39–44.
10 Roger G. Ibbotson. "The Importance of Asset Allocation," *Financial Analysts Journal*, Vol. 86, No. 2, 2010, pp. 18–20.
11 Ibid.
12 Benchmarks, such as the S&P 500, are used as proxies for "the market."
13 https://ycharts.com/indicators/sp_500_total_return_annual. Accessed February 10, 2020.
14 www.investopedia.com/articles/financial-theory/08/deeper-look-at-alpha.asp. Accessed November 22, 2019.
15 See, for example, Keith Ambachtsheer, "Alpha, Beta, Barrlegab: Investment theory of marketing strategy," in *Ambaschtsheer Letter*, April 2006.
16 Nicholas Rabener. "Warren Buffet: The Greatest Factor Investor of All Time." Available at: https://blogs.cfainstitute.org/investor/2019/04/15/warren-buffett-the-greatest-factor-investor-of-all-time/. Accessed February 16, 2020.
17 Thummin Cho. "Turning Alphas Into Betas: Arbitrage and Endogenous Risk," London School of Economics, October 2019.
18 Ibid. We also note the relevance of this academic research to the questions surrounding information efficiency, discussed in chapter 1.
19 See for example, www.msci.com/www/blog-posts/can-esg-add-alpha-/0182820893, accessed November 22, 2019; and Stephen Malinak and Shirley Birman. "Performance Tests of Truvalue Labs ESG as a 6th Factor", 2020, at: www.truvaluelabs.com/wp-content/uploads/2017/11/WP_PerfTest_SP500.pdf.
20 Gunnar Friede, Timo Busch, and Alexander Bassen. "ESG and Financial Performance: Aggregated Evidence from More than 2000 Empirical Studies" (October 22, 2015). *Journal of Sustainable Finance & Investment*, Vol. 5, Issue 4, pp. 210–233, 2015, DOI: 10.1080/20430795.2015.1118917. Available at SSRN: https://ssrn.com/abstract=2699610.
21 Witold Henisz, Tim Koller, and Robin Nuttall. "Five ways that ESG creates value," McKinsey Quarterly, November 2019. Available at: www.mckinsey.com/business-functions/strategy-and-corporate-finance/our-insights/five-ways-that-esg-creates-value?cid=soc-web&fbclid=IwAR3onKpp8NgbyctliHjvZHNs7HcqFUhaKamqMamTYZYE8eE4aC10BbRgm_U. Accessed November 22, 2019.
22 Witold J. Heinisz and James McGlinch, "ESG, Material Credit Events, and Credit Risk," *Journal of Applied Corporate Finance*, Vol. 31, Issue 2. Spring 2019, pp. 105–117.
23 Mozaffar N. Khan, George Serafeim, and Aaron Yoon. "Corporate Sustainability: First Evidence on Materiality." Harvard Business School Working Paper, No. 15–073, March 2015; "The Financial and Societal Benefits of ESG Integration: focus on materiality," Calvert Investments, June 2016; and "The Role of the Corporation in Society: implications for investors," Calvert Investments, September 2015.
24 Ola Mahmoud and Julia Meyer, "Sustainability in the Time of Uncertainty," May 2020 at: https://papers.ssrn.com/sol3/papers.cfm?abstract_id=3597700
25 George Serafeim and Aaron Yoon, "Does the Market React to Corporate ESG News?", Advance copy of paper provided to authors.
26 Costanza Consolandi, Robert G. Eccles, and Giampaolo Gabbi. "Better Fewer, But Better: Stock Returns and the Financial Relevance and Financial Intensity of Materiality," May 2020, at: https://papers.ssrn.com/sol3/papers.cfm?abstract_id=3574547
27 See, Ola Mahmoud and Julia Meyer. "Sustainability in the time of uncertainty," May, 2020, at: https://papers.ssrn.com/sol3/papers.cfm?abstract_id=3597700; and Alex Cheema-Fox, Bridget R. LaPerla, George Serafeim, and Hui (Stacie) Wang. "Corporate Resilience and Response during COVID-19," Harvard Working Paper Series No. 20–108.
28 *Op. cit.*, Friede et al.
29 Campbell R. Harvey and Yan Liu. *A Census of the Factor Zoo* (February 25, 2019). Available at SSRN: https://ssrn.com/abstract=3341728 or http://dx.doi.org/10.2139/ssrn.3341728.

30 John West and Alex Pickard, "Plausible Performance: Have Smart Beta Return Claims Jumped the Shark?", *Research Affiliates*, December 2019. Available at: www.researcha ffiliates.com/en_us/publications/articles/767-plausible-performance.html?evar36=eml_plau sible-performance-hero-title&_cldee=amx1a29tbmlrQHNpbmNsYWlyY2FwaXRhbC5 jb20%3d&recipientid=contact-2880b5f8c7cbe2119aa7005056bc3cff-42a2b5dbe4e24286a b95ff52b9ed24a9&esid=b3728812-e715-ea11-80e4-f24e75708764. Accessed December 19, 2019.

31 Julie Segal. "New SSGA Ron O'Hanley Says Asset Allocation Is the New Active," *Institutional Investor*, April 22, 2015.

32 Amar Bhidé. *A Call for Judgment: Sensible Finance for a Dynamic Economy*. Oxford University Press (2010), p. 116.

33 For example, Malinak and Berman. *Op cit.*, p. 6, Figure 2.

34 "Comptroller Stringer, NYC Pension Funds Launch National Campaign To Give Share-owners A True Voice In How Corporate Boards Are Elected," Press release, November 6, 2014. Accessible at https://comptroller.nyc.gov/newsroom/comptroller-stringer-nyc-p ension-funds-launch-national-campaign-to-give-shareowners-a-true-voice-in-how-corpora te-boards-are-elected. Accessed December 24, 2019.

35 Tara Bhandari, Peter Iliev, and Jonathan Kalodimos. "Governance Changes through Shareholder Initiatives: The Case of Proxy Access." (February 18, 2019). Fourth Annual Conference on Financial Market Regulation. Available at SSRN: https://ssrn. com/abstract=2635695 or http://dx.doi.org/10.2139/ssrn.2635695 Accessed December 24, 2019.

36 *Op cit.*, Comptroller Stringer press release of November 6, 2014.

37 *Op cit.* Bhandari *et al.*

38 Boardroom Accountability Project. Available at: https://comptroller.nyc.gov/services/ financial-matters/boardroom-accountability-project/overview. Accessed December 24, 2019.

39 Ibid.

40 Boardroom Accountability Project 2015 Company Focus List. Available at: https://comp troller.nyc.gov/wp-content/uploads/2014/11/Board-Room-Accountability-2015-Company-List.pdf. Accessed on December 27, 2019.

41 Public listed equities in the US aggregate market value was approximately $25 trillion at the time. Market capitalization of listed domestic companies (current US$), World Federation of Exchanges data. Available at: https://data.worldbank.org/indicator/ CM.MKT.LCAP.CD. Accessed December 27, 2017.

42 Tim Doyle. "Politics Over Performance, The Politicization of the New York City Retirement Systems," American Council for Capital Formation, January 2018. Available at: https://accfcorpgov.org/wp-content/uploads/2018/01/ACCF_New-York-City-Pension-Funds_FINAL.pdf. Accessed December 27, 2019.

43 The authors agree that "beta washing" is a theoretical problem. That is, investors could select issues of limited financial impact and dress them up as efforts to build better beta. However, we believe there are market mechanisms to prevent wide-spread adoption of beta-washed political campaigns. The more common risk is in the other direction: From blinkered proponents of traditional MPT who refuse to regard anything other than buying and selling securities as legitimate investment activities and therefore discourage activities that could materially benefit investors and society.

3 Short-termism

Short-Termism

There is nothing inherent in Modern Portfolio Theory (MPT) that would favor the short term over longer time frames. Indeed, by creating an intellectual paradigm that allows investors to more comfortably access riskier and longer-dated investments with cash flows extending far into the future (like equities), MPT should have helped to create a long-term investor mind-set. Yet for decades the academic literature and daily news reports have been awash with reports of "short-termism." The CFA Institute, which is the think tank of the accreditation body for hundreds of thousands of analysts and portfolio managers around the globe, even hosts a web page titled, simply, "short-termism." Here is what it writes:

> "Short-termism refers to an excessive focus on short-term results at the expense of long-term interests. Short-term performance pressures on investors can result in an excessive focus on their parts on quarterly earnings, with less attention paid to strategy, fundamentals and long-term value creation. Corporations too often respond to these pressures by reducing their expenditures on research and development and/or foregoing investment opportunities with positive long-term potential. These decisions can weigh against companies' development of sustainable products or investment in measures that deliver operational efficiencies, develop their human capital or effectively manage the social and environmental risks to their business."[1]

We believe that the CFA Institute is correct that investors often think irrationally about time frames. (By irrational, we mean that investors act in ways that are demonstrably contrary to their interests.) MPT is not the villain here, but neither is it an innocent bystander. Just as MPT does not cause systematic risk, but its lack of focus on a way to combat it creates the MPT paradox; so, too, MPT's focus on portfolio construction and its implication that trading activities are needed to do so does not cause short-termism, but it discourages the actions that could combat it and could contribute to the conditions that encourage short-termism.

Time-shifted rationality

Investors – and all human beings – are neurologically inclined to hyper-discount future events compared with those that are close in time. Hyper-discounting means irrationality, by definition, as the decision favors the near term over a justifiable discount given for the time delay and uncertainty of a later pay-off. Given that one aspect of markets is that they are discounting machines of future cash flows, this very human tendency looms large over how we make investment decisions. As BlackRock's CEO Larry Fink notes, "capital markets pull future risk forward."[2] The problem is that they pull it forward faster than they should.

The temporal trade-offs that humans make (eat now versus later, spend now versus save and spend later, etc.) have been studied extensively. A trio of Duke University researchers reviewed more than a dozen studies that used neuroimaging technology (functional magnetic resonance imaging, functional MRI) to see how brains respond to making temporal discounting decisions; that is, decisions about how to value something now versus something else later, which is what investors do when they use discount rates in analysis. They found that "distinct brain regions play important roles in intertemporal choice, compared to other forms of decision making."[3]

Why might this be important? In a keynote speech to a group of researchers examining investors' time horizons, Vanderbilt Professor Owen Jones notes that functional MRIs show a tension between activity in the limbic system, which is an ancient portion of our brains, and the pre-frontal cortex, a more recently evolved (in evolutionary terms) brain region. "The limbic areas of the brain are typically considered to be evolutionarily old – more emotional if you will, and with less cognitive and analytic capability than areas of the brain that evolved much later. Lower prefrontal cortex activity and greater limbic activity correlates with subjects biasing their choices toward the sooner, smaller reward. All this raises the hypothesis that there is some sort of a tension at work, when one is making time-discounting decisions, between the more analytic regions of the brain and the more emotional regions of the brain."[4]

Wilson suggests that irrational hyper-discounting might really be what he calls "time-shifted rationalities." In other words, what might be irrational today might have served a rational function at some evolutionary stage millions of years ago:

> The average lifespan was much shorter than it is today. Our ancestors were also less likely to reach the maximum lifespan than you are to approach it (at least in high-wealth countries) in the modern era. Also, trade was quite risky. Why? Because our deep ancestors had no robust enforcement mechanisms. Secure rights were limited to what you had in your hand (if you were lucky) or to what you could store around your belly through immediate consumption. Trade was risky in the following sense: you have got something over which you have dominion, and you are considering trading it for something else that you might want more, but which you

might have a very small chance of actually getting in return for what you relinquish. For this reason, we can hypothesize that, throughout primate history (indeed for the vast bulk of all organisms), natural selection will have favored heritable predispositions to weigh the concrete present somewhat more heavily than the theoretical future.

We can cognitively control some of our investment behavior by reflecting on it and becoming educated about it. But our basic behavioral predispositions are encountering novel environmental features. And the result of that encounter will often lead to some weird outcomes in the modern era."[5]

In addition to the differences between our evolutionary programming and the realities of the "modern era" that Wilson cites, there is another contextual conundrum. Our thinking about temporal discounting is based on our being human, which means that we are mortal and have a finite time in this world. But institutional investors are often making temporal decisions for eternally lived entities, such as pension funds, endowments, collective investment funds, insurance companies, and the like. Those entities should be focused very long-term.

Wilson's theories suggest a biologic factor contributing to prospect theory, the founding touchstone of behavioral finance. Kahneman and Twersky suggest that people fear loss of what they have more than they desire future gains. Loss-aversion – which our stressed ancestors would have well understood – seems to dominate over "rational" equal weighting of risks, whether positive or negative.

Hyper-discounting, Investing, and Public Policy

These tendencies to hyper-discount and to be loss-avverse have real-world impact. As Bank of England Chief Economist Andrew Haldane notes, "cash-flows 5 years ahead are discounted at rates more appropriate (to) 8 or more years hence; 10 year ahead cash-flows are valued as if 16 or more years ahead; and cash-flows more than 30 years ahead are scarcely valued at all. The long is short. Investment choice, like other life choices, is being re-tuned to a shorter wave-length."[6]

Haldane, like the CFA Institute, also notes that the tendency to hyper-discount means that investments with long-term positive societal and economic impacts do not get the amount of investment that they deserve. "This is a market failure. It would tend to result in investment being too low and in long-duration projects suffering disproportionately. This might include projects with high build or sunk costs, including infrastructure and high-tech investments. These projects are often felt to yield the highest long-term (private and social) returns and hence offer the biggest boost to future growth." As a regulator, Haldane is well aware of the intermediation purpose of investment, so notes that not only does hyper-discounting result in sub-optimal investing decisions, but also in sub-optimal capital allocation. "That makes short-termism a public policy issue," he concludes.[7]

However, a decade after Haldane's call to action, not much has changed. There are myriad investor and business groups that agitate for long-term capital deployment, but neither they nor regulators and lawmakers have managed to have the markets revalue future cash flows to be more fairly discounted. And the increasing portion of the real economy which flows through the capital markets – the so-called financialization of the economy – exacerbates the impacts of the hyper-discounting market failure.

Perhaps the advocates for long-termism are thinking about it wrongly. They continuously make the (correct) intellectual arguments. But something seems to act as a barrier to those arguments taking root and branching out throughout the marketplace. Wilson argues that we can "cognitively control some of our investment behavior." But if the tendency to hyper-discount can be overridden with focus and dedication, then why do we not do so? (That we do not seems to be settled: Haldane's cash flow analyses prove that, as a rule, investors do not.) We postulate that part of the barrier is the role MPT plays in today's capital markets.

Think about what conditions cause emotional reactions and which encourage thoughtful analysis. Being faced with limited time, multiple confusing choices, stress, and limited knowledge often results in emotional decisions, in which we revert, at best, to heuristics and, at worst, to jumping to a conclusion. By contrast, time to contemplate, a simple set of choices, a calm environment, and detailed knowledge allows rational analysis. Which describes a portfolio manager today? Some investors try to take "emotion" out of the process through programmatic trading. But those algorithms – while helpful – are not perfect. First, they are programmed by humans, so human biases are included. The amount of price movement necessary to trigger a trade might already reflect hyper-discounting. To paraphrase the famous garbage-in-garbage-out warning, short-term-bias-input = short-term-bias-output. Second, they are employed to achieve the trading firm's goals, and the overall pressure to differentiate over periods as short a calendar quarter remains. So why would they be programmed for long-termism? Third, algorithms generally are based on price and volume, which means that other, non-programmatic traders can cause price movements to which the trading programs must react. Even when algorithmic trading is not based on price, it is still often focused on the short term. For example, trading programs can be based on using bots to scrape news feeds and social media for instant information.

The MPT tradition in recent decades of focusing on alpha-seeking and the asset management industry's need for differentiation among active managers creates conditions that encourage frequent trading on imperfect knowledge. Those are conditions that facilitate, rather than discourage, hyper-discounting. In the most frenzied markets, when decisions are most important, conditions are even worse for rational decision-making.

The focus on alpha and beating benchmarks contributes to portfolio managers trying to distinguish themselves from their competitors by trading, as the differential impact of such trading on a portfolio compared with peers and the benchmark manifests immediately. The availability of instant analyses and the use of relatively short comparison periods – portfolios tend to be judged on one-quarter, one-year and three-year relative return statistics – provides reinforcement for differentiated short-term results. Market structural changes, which increased efficiency in trading, a good thing for price discovery, had an unintentional impact of decreasing the transaction costs of acting in a short-term manner. Among those changes were: decimalization of trading, lower trading costs, unbundling of execution-only trading from bundled services such as research, technologic advances such as algorithmic trading and trading bots, low-fee retail trading access, trading via mobile apps, etc. Again, these have very positive impacts in reducing costs. But they also decrease the friction that helped to decrease frequent trading and short-termism. When you combine all those things, the resulting cultural pressure of the industry to trade is intense. There is, as one study put it, a "don't just sit there, do something imperative."[8] The result is that most portfolio managers trade even more than they, themselves expect. And they do so even though they know, intellectually, that the frictional costs of trading, as well as the distractions of constantly changing their portfolios, probably negatively affects their returns.[9]

As the CFA Institute writes: "There's… tension with the owners of the money being managed, who often require a long-term investment view (a retirement fund, for example). As a result of this misalignment of interests between the two groups, significant losses for investors can arise. Transaction costs aggravate this problem; because a short-term outlook often drives high portfolio turnover, this can lead to high transaction costs, reducing returns to investors."[10]

The numbers bear this out. According to the World Federation of Exchanges, the annual turnover of an average stock increased from less than 40 percent in 1975 to more than 100 percent in 2018.[11] Put another way, the holding period decreased from more than two-and-a-half years to less than one year. And while so-called high-frequency trading (the use of computer programs to trade on price anomalies on a millisecond basis) surely contributes to that, alternative measures of investor time horizons which do not involve high-frequency trading also indicate that investors turn over their portfolios every 18 months or so.[12] Interestingly, the professors who developed that measure found that the average stock duration had increased marginally, from 1.2 to 1.5 years in the quarter century ended 2010, driven largely by an increased duration by pension funds, which have been among the loudest critics of short-termism. The very same researchers also found that investors who trade less frequently actually perform better.[13]

That makes sense. If, on average, investors irrationally hyper-discount when analyzing a potential trade, then trading less frequently would have two complementary and salutary effects. First, taking more time for analysis of each decision should allow more pre-frontal cortex analytical activity. Second, even if hyper-discounting among infrequent traders occurs at the same level generally, the lesser frequency of trading means that irrationality will be multiplied fewer times, making infrequent traders "less wrong" than the market as a whole, causing outperformance.

Do We Measure the Right Things?

There is another issue about short-termism, which is rarely examined: *Are we even measuring investor horizons correctly?* MPT's focus on alpha and relative returns achieved through analysis and trading means that we measure the holding period (or other temporal measure) of a stock or bond or other security, because we want to measure the return of that security, or a portfolio, against "the market." As with relative performance metrics, holding period for a specific stock or a specific portfolio of securities is an internal metric of the capital markets, not a measure of how investors think about, or act with regard to, capital markets. The simple truth is that most investors are permanently exposed to the market and therefore to the systematic and idiosyncratic risks that comprise it. Very few, if any, investors go from not investing to buying a security and then back to not investing.[14] Rather, the proceeds from the sale of one security typically are used to purchase another security. Put another way, virtually all investors have permanent exposure to systematic market risk, which will still determine 75–95 percent of their return. For the vast majority of capital invested, it does not matter if the fund through which it gains market exposure has a holding period of a day, a year, or a decade; the actual period of exposure to beta is probably forever. However, as noted above, frequent traders[15] have costs greater than the market as a whole and are exposed to time-shifted rationality and loss-aversion behavioral issues more often than other market participants. So, if a fund trades multiples more frequently than the market average, you can expect degraded performance on average.

On a more macro level, to the extent that the market as a whole continues to become more short-term vis-à-vis individual securities, the performance degrading aspects of trading increasingly affect the risk/return of the entire market. Also, from an intermediation and societally efficient allocation of capital point of view, to the extent "short-termism is a public policy issue,"[16] it is one that is increasing in impact, owing both to the exacerbation of the underlying hyper-discounting and to the increased amount of the real economy that flows through the capital markets ("financialization").

The overriding point is that most investors have permanent beta exposure. Holding periods and stock duration measure trades, not investors' time horizons. So, for example, many exceptionally long-term investors such as endowments or pension funds invest through index funds both for their low cost and what these investors perceive as index funds' long-term market exposure. However, as the authors have noted previously, at least for traditionally constructed capitalization-weighted indices, "the index investor is exposed to short-term, relative return thinking via the index construction rules that reflect the market's trading activity. Indeed, some have called capitalization-weighted indices covert "momentum" style vehicles, as a price gain for a stock (disproportionate to the rest of the index universe) increases its weight in the index. Cap-weighted indices are, effectively, price takers. If (too many) price makers are short-term, then price takers/indices reflect this (and perhaps magnify it due to the index effect). The irony here is that dedicated long-term passive owners may own long-term, but do not determine or influence capitalization of what they own. Short-term alpha-seeking sets the parameters for these beta-trackers."[17] This is the long-term dog being wagged by the short-term tail.

This, then, is a formula for a short-term oriented market:

Alpha-seeking trading increasing in frequency
+ Hyper-discounting of future cash flows in those trades due to time-shifted rationality
+ Capitalization-weighted indices with weights determined by those making hyper-discounted alpha-seeking trades
+ Increased popularity of those capitalization-weighted strategies
= Market driven by irrational short-termism

Notes

1 www.cfainstitute.org/en/advocacy/issues/short-termism. Accessed January 24, 2020.
2 www.blackrock.com/corporate/investor-relations/larry-fink-ceo-letter. Accessed February 12, 2020.
3 R. McKell Carter, Justin R. Meyer, and Scott A. Huettel. "Functional Neuroimaging of Intertemporal Choice Models: A Review". *Journal of Neuroscience, Psychology and Economics*; 2010, Vol. 3, No. 1, pp. 27–45.
4 Jones, Owen D. Keynote address: Brain Science Perspectives on Investor Behavior and Decision-Making Errors (June 1, 2017). *Seattle University Law Review*, Vol. 41, pp. 349–366, 2018; Vanderbilt Law Research Paper No. 18–22. Jones, Owen D. Keynote Address: Brain Science Perspectives on Investor Behavior and Decision-Making Errors (June 1, 2017). *Seattle University Law Review*, Vol. 41, pp. 349–366, 2018, Vanderbilt Law Research Paper No. 18–22, Available at SSRN: https://ssrn.com/abstract=3168062.
5 Ibid.
6 Andrew G. Haldane and Richard Davies. "The Short Long," Speech before the 29th Société Universitaire Européenne de Recherches Financières Colloquium, New Paradigm in Money and Finance? May 2011.
7 Haldane, Ibid.
8 Danyelle Guyat and Jon Lukomnik. "Does Portfolio Turnover Exceed Expectations?", *Rotman International Journal of Pension Management*, Vol. 3, No. 2, Fall 2010.
9 Ibid.
10 www.cfainstitute.org/en/advocacy/issues/short-termism. Accessed January 24, 2020.
11 https://data.worldbank.org/indicator/CM.MKT.TRNR. Accessed January 3, 2020.
12 Martijn Cremers, Ankur Pareet, and Andreas Sautner, *Stock Duration and Misvaluation*, Working Paper, University of Amsterdam (2013).
13 See, for example, K. Cremers, J. Martijn, and Ankur Pareek. "Patient Capital Outperformance: The Investment Skill of High Active Share Managers Who Trade Infrequently (December 1, 2015)," *Journal of Financial Economics*. Forthcoming. Available at SSRN: https://ssrn.com/abstract=2498743 or http://dx.doi.org/10.2139/ssrn.2498743.
14 Investors who do try to time the market tend to fare badly. See, for example, Ilia D. Dichev, "What are Stock Investors' Actual Historical Returns? Evidence from

Dollar-Weighted Returns." 2 (December 2004). Available at: https://ssrn.com/abstra ct=544142. Accessed February 12, 2020. Dichev finds that dollar weighted returns are systematically lower than buy-and-hold returns, by more than 1% a year.

15 In this context we consider frequent traders to be human or quantitative traders exercising stock-picking analytics, not high-frequency traders exploiting price anomalies.

16 Haldane, *Op cit*.

17 Jim Hawley and Jon Lukomnik. "The Long and Short of It: Are We Asking the Right Questions?" *Seattle University Law Review*, Vol. 41, Issue 2, 2018.

4   Everything Old Is New Again

Everything Old Is New Again: Feedback Loops and Becoming Material

Arguing that Modern Portfolio Theory (MPT) is artificial in viewing investing as disjointed from the various causes of value creation can be seen as innovative, even radical. But it reflects classical economics' concern with the feedback loops that affect and evolve economic decision-making. The need to examine the relationship of economics to the real world outside of financial markets and how they interact has been studied by economists as varied as Adam Smith, Karl Marx, Ronald Coase, Oliver Williamson, and Milton Friedman,

Although coming from very different suppositions and approaches, the commonality of these seminal thinkers is that they suggest that our critique of MPT for artificially separating markets from the broader economy is not new, but rather a contemporary application of traditional examinations of complex causes, constraints, incentives, and feedbacks. Our criticism is less new thinking than remembering a past too often forgotten and in urgent need of resurrection.

Adam Smith

Adam Smith viewed self-interest and sympathy for fellow human beings as complementary, not antithetical. He writes: "This disposition to admire, and almost to worship, the rich and the powerful, and to despise, or, at least, to neglect persons of poor and mean condition, though necessary both to establish and to maintain the distinction of ranks and the order of society, is, at the same time, the great and most universal cause of the corruption of our moral sentiments."[1] And similarly: "As society cannot subsist unless the laws of justice are tolerably observed, as no social intercourse can take place among men who do not generally abstain from injuring one another..."[2] Core to both ideas is that society (read morality and law) needs to channel and contain the rather simple minded interpretation of the pure economic self (too often read as selfish) interest of Smith's famous butcher, baker, and brewer in *The Wealth of Nations*. Smith makes that clear in *The Theory of Moral Sentiments*, when he writes: "When we consider the character of any individual, we naturally view it under two different aspects; first, as it may affect his own happiness; and secondly, as it may affect that of other people."

Certainly Smith viewed the broader society as a constraint on the actions available to fulfill self-interest: "Society cannot subsist among those who are ready to hurt one another."[3] But perhaps more interestingly, he makes it clear that the feedback loop from society to individual also affects what is best for the individual, not just what is allowable. "Concern for our own happiness recommends to us the virtue of prudence: concern for that of other people, the virtues of justice and beneficence; of which, the one restrains us from hurting, the other prompts us to promote that happiness. Independent of any regard either to what are, or to what ought to be, or to what upon a certain condition would be, the sentiments of other people, the first of those three virtues is originally recommended to us by our selfish, the other two by our benevolent affections."[4]

In short, Smith harmonized two seemingly contradictory sentiments (social psychological impulses); those of self-interest and benevolence. Society constrains self-interest, but also informs it. An individual's economic decisions result from the interplay of that duality.

Ronald Coase

Nobel Prize-winning economist Ronald Coase's main focus was mitigating negative externalities at the least economy-wide cost. Coase's main ideas have over time been selectively distorted by hard free market theorists to argue against all or most government regulation. They argue that leaving problems to the market can achieve socially optimal mitigation without (too much) regulation. In this idealized, *laissez-faire* world, costless bargaining would lead to socially efficient solutions absent regulation (although not absent contract and other aspects of law). However, that politically driven reading of Coase ignores a key aspect of his writings. He specifies the assumptions necessary for *laissez-faire* solutions and makes clear that they are so restrictive and unrealistic that they are more thought experiment than prescription for a durable economic system. Indeed, Coase himself said as much. Williamson, as discussed below, suggests that in some regards Coase (and more, his followers) overplay the "marvels of the market" argument by not examining the transaction costs of contracting.[5]

There are many reasons that costless bargaining is between rare and non-existent. Among the most important impediments are imperfect and/or asymmetrical information and cheating (politely called opportunism) to name two important ones. Others include resources, power imbalances, expertise, and risk-aversion.

Another situation limiting the ability to simply rely upon market forces as the optimal economic decision-maker is if there are many parties involved in a transaction, and/or many variables to take into account, as this raises transactions costs to often absurd levels. In such cases, Coase clearly recognized that government action could be the least costly alternative to private ordering. Automobile pollution is a case in point: Hundreds of millions of parties (automobile users) and limitless geographical points make negotiation impossible. Even if negotiations were theoretically possible, their transition costs would far outweigh whatever inefficiencies might come from government regulation. Thus, while Coase's abstract system appeals to free market advocates, he has clear – and many – parameter limits. Indeed, a careful reading of Coase suggests that where there are significant externalities, transactional costs, or the inability to rely on costless bargaining, markets fail.

While clearly a proponent of markets, what is really interesting and important about Coase is the clear recognition of the limits of his abstract system, from the real world complexity which creates impediments to reliance on market solutions to the externalities which affect those not directly involved in the costless bargaining, even if such market-based economic decision-making would be possible. In the closing comments of his famous 1960 social costs article, Coase wrote: "…it is, of course, desirable that the choice between different social arrangements for the solution of economic problems should be carried out in broader terms than [narrow economic factor focus].that the total effect of these arrangement in all spheres of life should be taken into account." He concludes by quoting economist Frank Knight that, "…problems of welfare economics must ultimately dissolve into a study of aesthetics and morals."[6] Coase thus closes the circle back to Smith's moral sentiments. Moreover, as neither aesthetics nor morals are fixed in stone, considering them creates an ever-evolving set of conversations about what is acceptable, useful and even what is efficient. In other words, the real world and Coase's optimized ideal of costless bargaining are engaged in a perpetual feedback loop, with both influencing the other, to determine what is an efficient answer to an economic issue at a particular time, in a particular place, affecting a particular set of participants.

Coase's acknowledgement of limitations to, and problems with, purely market-based solutions stands in stark contrast to Markowitz's original work and to others' view of MPT where the abstract system is practically self-enclosed, with the only feedback mechanism from the real world being the price of a security. That is a very small window for feedback from a very complicated set of systems.

Oliver Williamson

Williamson, another Nobel Prize winner, explicitly rejected the neoclassic economic tradition, which was "dismissive of institutions" replacing it with New Institutional Economics (NIE).[7] NIE explicitly links its "institutions matter" belief with those elements in Smith and Coase who, whatever their differences, in their own ways focus on institutions mattering.

MPT, in its origins and in its subsequent development, ignores institutions mattering. This is ironic; its massive success performatively laid the basis for new institutions (e.g. index funds, the massive growth of institutional investors). And of course, MPT embedded itself within then existing institutions as both a belief system and a set of value extraction techniques. Being, as we have argued, a victim of its own success, MPT's blinders about institutions mattering has restricted MPT's proponents from critically thinking about its own institutions.

Williamson's work – notably his creation of transaction cost economics (TCE) – is a masterful antidote to this self-imposed MPT blindness. Williamson is explicitly interdisciplinary, moving between economics and organizational theory. Much of his work focuses on governance, a quintessential essence of institutions, on social impacts on those institutions, and on how economics shape the institutions. TCE – Williamson's examination of how institutions transact most efficiently – is linked explicitly to changes in the larger social world. Williamson writes: "If changes in property rights, contract laws, norms, customs, and the like induce changes in the comparative [transactions] costs of governance, then a re-configuration of economic organization is usually implied."[8] Williamson's focus on governance flows from Coase's theory of the firm, but Williamson brilliantly evolves our understanding, from the firm as an unexamined black box "production function" in the neo-classical economics paradigm to a knowable intersection of governance and hierarchy. He suggests the neo-classical economics, and implicitly therefore MPT, focuses on the science of choice in allocating scarce resources. In contrast, NIE/TCE focuses on the study of contracts, which includes both public and private ordering, both of which have governance as their centerpiece, as both are forms of hierarchy.[9] More specifically, Williamson suggests that, "TCE shares a good deal of common ground with game theory …in that the parties to a contract are assumed to have an understanding of the strategic situation within which they are located and position themselves accordingly. TCE nonetheless differs in that contractual incompleteness sets in as the limits on rationality become binding in relation to transactional complexity."[10]

Like Coase and Smith before him, the role of culture and human impulses and cognition are central, which flows from Williamson's view on organizational theory.

Milton Friedman

At first glance it might seem odd to include Milton Friedman, godfather of *laissez-faire* capitalism, in our list of major thinkers whose work reveals MPT's limitations. A quick focus on his hugely influential New York Times essay *The social responsibility of business is to increase profits*, published 50 years ago at the time of writing, suggests that Friedman understood, as Smith and others before him, what he called the basic "rules of society, both those embodied in law and those embodied in ethical custom" as critical to economic action.[11] While ethical custom and law are entirely unexamined by Friedman, it is nonetheless exactly parallel to Smith's moral sentiments and to what both Coase and Williamson focused on, especially the later. Neither law nor ethical custom are fixed; they change over time, differ place to place, and have huge import on economic organization and function.

Yet Friedman's model of capitalism and corporations, unlike Smith's or Williamson's, did entirely ignore the massive agency issue at the heart of governance generally and corporate governance specifically. This is well captured when he wrote, "...the manager is the agent of the individuals who own the corporation" and that the manager (read CEO) is "selected by the stockholders." Even for 1970, that was a remarkably naïve statement. Therefore, it is no surprise that Friedman, like Markowitz and others of his contemporaries embedded in the neo-classical paradigm, ignored not only Smith on agency theory, but most importantly the work of Berle and Means from the 1930s through the 1960s, among many others.[12] However, whatever the critical failure of Friedman to recognize the problem of agency opportunism and the incentives for executive rent-seeking inherent in the corporate form, it is nonetheless important to understand that at least in theory he recognized the importance of ethical custom. Indeed, even the key sentence that advocates of market-based, *laissez-faire* capitalism cite the most from that essay – "there is one and only one social responsibility of business – to use its resources and engage in activities designed to increase its profits" ends with a caveat that recognizes that society constrains economically "rational" self-interest impulses. He finishes with "so long as it stays within the rules of the game, which is to say, engages in open and free competition without deception or fraud."[13] An important caveat: As Duncan Austin points out, there is what he called a "Friedman's feedback loop" which is that if the social responsibility of business to make profits, then part of making profits entails activities such as political lobbying, regulatory capture, and the like, in order to influence and/or dominate the "rules of the game" processes and institutions. Such activities might often result in greater profits, regardless of the negative externality effects resulting from such rules or lack thereof. This of course might well and often has vitiated customary norms and rules, which never have existed apart from social dynamics.[14]

Friedman wrote that essay from the perspective of the company, not from that of investors. But we can suppose minimal semantic changes to translate his theory to investors: "There is one and only one social responsibility of investors – to use their resources and engage in activities designed to increase returns so long as they stay within the rule of the game..." Yet, transposing Friedman's perspective from that of a business to that of investors suggests a huge, even fundamental, change. It would give investors latitude to try to impact businesses towards considering systemic impacts so as to mitigate systematic risks for investors. Such actions are both profit (or returns) seeking, and within the rules of the game. Therefore, Friedman would say that such activity was the "social responsibility" of investors. There would then be a market-based dynamic at work between Friedman's imperative for business – increasing profits and the one for investors, increasing returns. Those two imperatives are neither necessarily oppositional nor synchronous. But they do underscore that Friedman's "rules of the game" are a more essential and complicated part of that sentence than generally considered.

Also, were Friedman writing today, the rules of the game would be very different from 1970. Would Friedman have recognized that businesses affect the world around them, which then affects those businesses and so on in a cyclical feedback, meaning the rules of the game – determined by the "ethical custom" of the age – have evolved? For instance, in 1970 businesses' senior management were almost exclusively white and male. Today, that is considered a missed opportunity to benefit from a larger opportunity set of talent, and to realize the benefits of diverse viewpoints in the executive suite. Certainly, even in 1970 Friedman would not have supported maximizing profits through the use of slavery or piracy or feudal serfdom, because the rules of that era had already eliminated those practices (or at least made them abhorrent and illegal in widespread practice). Thus, his caveats about the rules of the game cannot be ignored, and, over time, the rules of the game change. Indeed, sometimes the game itself changes, or there are multiple, overlapping games being played.

Karl Marx

If, as noted in chapter 1, the MPT revolution has, at least partly, eaten its own children, what better economist to examine so as to understand why than Karl Marx. While Smith, Coase, Williamson, and even, to some extent, Friedman, write about the real world's ever-evolving constraints, influences, and feedbacks to economic decision-making, Marx focuses on something different: The impact of theory itself being widely accepted.

Writing some 50 years after Smith, Marx suggests that ideas (theory) are a powerful force, once widely believed, which influence economic decisions. "The weapon of criticism cannot, of course, replace criticism by weapons, material force must be overthrown by material force; but theory also becomes a material force as soon as it has gripped the masses. Theory is capable of gripping the masses as soon as it demonstrates *ad hominem*, and it demonstrates *ad hominem* as soon as it becomes radical."[15] The Russian Revolution nearly three quarters of a century later, based, at least theoretically, on the adoption (or perhaps mis-adoption) of his Marx's own theories, proved just how prescient Marx was in predicting that theory can become force.

In its own way, MPT was nothing if not radical. It became, as we have noted previously, "performative," or as Marx would have said, a "material force," in that its widespread adoption changed marketplace behavior. Unlike Marx, however, MPT does not acknowledge that theory can change context. One result of that is that MPT has no way to deal with the fact that its widespread adoption has created new and problematic issues.

As different as they are, Smith, Coase, Williamson, Friedman, and even Marx never lose sight of the relation of economy, society, and theory to individual decision, nor the fact that "moral sentiments," "ethical customs," the "rules of the game," and accepted theory change over time, resulting in changing economic decision-making. By contrast, MPT's singular focus directly flows from the neo-classical economic tradition which posits *homo economicus* (economic human) as statically and permanently motivated by a single force of economic "rationality" resulting in a simplistic utilitarian and self-centered calculation unfettered by society and unaffected by its changes over time. MPT implicitly rejects that context and consequences are relevant and that those changes create feedback loops between the market's economic decision-making and the non-market world. It is as if MPT believes that financial markets exist in a vacuum and assume that the resultant outcomes will be automatically broadly beneficial to the real world and to the systems on which the economy and society depend. Not only is it a fundamentally constrained vision, ignoring Coase's more nuanced understanding of when market-based solutions are unworkable, it is also a static one, silent as to how investors should (and do) evolve over time. In this way it rejects the lessons not only of Coase, but also Smith, Marx, Williamson, Friedman, and myriad other economists, as well as the behavioralists (e.g. Twersky and Kahneman) discussed in chapter 1.

The only way to square that circle is by assuming that price is a perfect conductor of all the complexities of the world and synchronously reacts as the world evolves; that there is perfect and symmetric information which is universally understood; that discount rates are rational; that nobody has preferences for the types of risk that they undertake based either on their institutional needs or moral or religious preferences, so that volatility is all that matters, and on and on and on. You have to believe all that to believe that MPT perfectly incorporates changing ethical norms, moral sentiments, and rules of the game. That is a huge burden for the slender reed of price. Yet, some might argue that such perfect conditions need not exist; that the imperfections are what creates the market. But these imperfections are not the normal "different market participants having different calculations of value" but are actually some of the limitations that Coase suggests mark when costless bargaining is impaired, and markets are not efficient for society.

Ethical Norms, Material Forces, and Materiality

Viewed with historical distance and perspective, the connections between norms, law, regulation, and market behavior are quite apparent. What is considered in one place and time as socially (market) acceptable changes over time and location, sometimes slowly and sometimes quite rapidly. Slavery, while always controversial among non-slaves (and hardly controversial among enslaved people), was part and parcel of early capitalism, but eventually made illegal (although we note that quasi-slave and clandestine practices continue). The same with child labor, labor health and safety standards, hours of work, discrimination (e.g. age, race, gender, sexual orientation), and a host of other issues. Markets adjust eventually, albeit both unevenly and far from in a straight line. The actual behavior of individual firms and investors is typically both faster and slower than the codification of those newly evolved market norms into law and regulation. Law and regulation tend to be both binary and universal within the jurisdiction. That is, a practice either is or is not allowed upon effective date of the changed legal status. By contrast, some of the market will have shifted in advance of the legal change, reflecting the evolving consensus as to market norms which probably contributed to the legal status change. That consensus is neither universal nor instantaneous, however, and for those firms and investors that had shifted in advance, the legal change was slow. For those firms and investors who cling to the old social norms past the effective date (creating regulatory risk) the change came too fast. Those lagging market players sometimes complain that they are being penalized for doing what they have always done, and that the rules have shifted under them. They are correct: Shifting societal values cause shifting laws reflecting shifting beliefs about what creates value and risk.

Of course, norms are not just about ethics and morality, but encompass all evolutions in what society considers as acceptable behavior. Our improved understanding of science also forces investors, firms, and the public to confront those insights. For example, it had been known for millennia that ground water can be contaminated, thereby impacting not just the ecosystem, but production and livelihoods that depend on potable and useful water. However, as those understandings deepened and changed, new norms of behavior developed. From these, new regulatory and legal standards developed, most typically in the face of intense opposition of the polluting firms.

How is this related to MPT's vision of the world? It is not, which is a problem.

MPT's static and encapsulated math makes it a screened-off entity within a detached economic paradigm, doubly isolated from the messy, but real, world of changing norms, of moral sentiment, and material forces. As MPT does not have theory nor empirics to consider how value is created (as opposed to using price as a metric to efficiently extract value through portfolio construction), it is not surprising that it is blind as to the interplay and the evolution from Value (ethical norms, moral sentiments) to value. Put another way, MPT is an instantaneous "as if" theoretical framing; it takes what is given without care as to where value has come from or is going to and without regard to its own contributions to values or devaluation. It assumes that the efficient market hypothesis means that all relevant information about value creation or destruction is contained in the price metric.

Materiality is Not a "State of Being" But a "State of Becoming"

Behavioral norms, when codified, become, in the words of Friedman, "the rules of the game." Those "rules" impact risk and return, the interrelation of firms and sectors (and thereby productivity), and, in the broadest sense, the social and environmental "commons." Unlike Smith, Coase, Marx, Williamson, and Friedman, MPT takes all of this as a given. The performative aspects of MPT blinkers investors to the impacts of their investments on the social "commons," the societal perception of "Values," and on investment returns themselves (focusing, as it does, on returns relative to the market, rather than returns relative to the investor's needs). The feedback loops between the market – particularly its capital allocation and governance functions – and its impacts upon the real world are beyond MPT's range of vision. MPT does not question whether it might itself play a role, positive or negative, in the Values to value dynamic through its impact on those financial markets and their subsequent impact on the world. The 1970s view about exclusionary screens might seem discordant, insensitive, and shortsighted today, but it was and is consistent with MPT's field of vision: If capital markets support apartheid today, but will not tomorrow, so be it. We have prices today and assume that they accurately reflect a discounted tomorrow.

MPT, by limiting its feedback to and from the real world to price, and by focusing on relative returns, rather than seeking to improve total market return by engaging with the sources of value and risk, is not neutral in the Values to value dynamic. MPT is accepting of, and therefore unintendedly complicit with, the real-world consequences of investors following its precepts.

The idea that price is an efficient single-point feedback mechanism goes beyond even the assumptions of a perfectly efficient market, with perfect information dissemination, no hyper-discounting of future cash flows, no pricing friction, etc. Even if you assume all that, price, because it is a market-clearing transaction, is a summary metric. Therefore, it simply cannot convey the various complex dynamics of the Values to value dynamic which includes those market players who, for whatever reason, do not seek to transact at that price at that time, or of stakeholders outside the market, but who still participate in the Values to value evolution through contributing to societal norms through non-market activities, which then might have an impact on the market, which, in turn, affects societal norms, which....

Values, during the period when they are coalescing into societal norms, have traditionally been labeled as "non-financial" or "extra-financial." A better term, which has been in use since about 2010, might be "not-yet-financial," making it clear that norm shifts and new understandings once adopted by a critical mass of investors, firms, the general population, regulators, become financially relevant. In financial and legal terms, they became material.[16]

This general process underlying what is and what is not considered to be material has often been described as the social construction of markets and has been widely studied by sociologists, anthropologists, economists, organizational theorists, and others.[17] Our focus here, however, is limited to how and why financial markets come to see what had previously been considered irrelevant or tangential as financially material, recognized sometimes as legally material, and how ignoring this dynamic is one of MPT's inadequacy. We will often use environmental, social, and governance (ESG) data as examples.

The evolution of human knowledge and beliefs means that the specifics of what is material (either as reflected in market practice or in law and regulatory mandate) have always been in flux. But today, what is in flux is even how we recognize what is material. The emergence of big data analytics creates the ability to trace changes in significant sentiment in real time. While it is still early days for this technology, initial reports suggest that it could identify what is material at a specific moment for an individual security, company, sector, or the market as a whole. It could also, within limits, suggest probabilistic trends for what might be material in the future.[18] Rogers and Serafeim write, "...there is a misperception that there is a bright line between material issues and immaterial ones…. externalities can be internalized [within the firm] when subject to the pressures of stakeholders, regulators or industry disruption."[19] Materiality from this perspective is not a state of being but a process of becoming over time. The processes that Rogers and Serafeim suggest that allow this to happen are similar to those outlined by economists from Smith to Friedman earlier in this chapter: When firm practices and social norms diverge enough there is a catalyst for the becoming material process. Stakeholder (including investor) reaction to these changes then takes center stage. In turn, companies often, but far from always, respond if they perceive their interests and reputations threatened. Finally, in some cases there are regulatory actions to codify or otherwise make changes in what is considered material.

This social construction of materiality approach can be tracked, measured, and, to a degree, predicted, using big data analytics. A World Economic Forum paper published in early 2020 makes a point similar to Rogers and Serafeim, noting that the pressures for corporate standardized disclosure, specifically in line with Sustainability Accounting Standards Board (SASB) and the Task Force on Climate-related Financial Disclosure, is enabled by a variety of technologies (e.g. satellite imaging of carbon emissions; text-based big data analytics by third parties using artificial intelligence and natural language processing). Firms no longer control or dominate information about their own behavior as much as they once did, although investors still need better and complete corporate-supplied information that is material today and information about issues likely to be material tomorrow. Underlying the parallel growth of stakeholder (and institutional asset manager and owner) involvement is a growing concern about negative externalities, and how they affect growing sectors of the economy and society, as well as the health of financial markets overall and their own diversified portfolios. There is increasing evidence that the convergence of these forces is powerful and likely to be here in the long term.[20]

One big data provider, Truvalue Labs, a Factset company (Disclosure: Hawley is Head of Applied Research at, and Lukomnik has been an advisor to Truvalue Labs), tracks, in real time, stakeholder data (global, national, and local media; non-government organization and stakeholder reports, etc.) using elements of artificial intelligence (e.g. national language processing, machine learning), enabling it to quantify unstructured, text-based data. A Truvalue Labs study that back-tested its data against the factors that SASB defines as material by industry and sector found a number of noteworthy trends. Looking at case studies of the semiconductor and oil and gas sectors, the study found that materiality was fluid and changed over time (from 2009 to 2019). Secondly, the back-tested data and analysis predicted which factors SASB would, years later, come to define as material. We note that SASB's consultative process was time-, labor- and cost-intensive, and quite comprehensive: SASB used stakeholder expert groups, open hearings, and comment periods, intensive human-based research and had thousands of participants. TVL's use of big data analysis of stakeholder text data resulted in the same outcome, with less cost, time, and labor. That is not to say that such big data analytics can substitute for the more traditional process.

Among the advantages of the SASB process is that it socializes determination of materiality as it occurs. More importantly, the fact that materiality is a social construct requires an affirmation by investors and other stakeholders to concretize what is or is not considered material at a specific point in time and for a specific market, industry, or company, lest the big data analytics make false projections. But the TVL analysis does suggest that big data analytics, at least in some cases, can spotlight those issues to which market participants are increasingly paying attention. It suggests that such analyses can be the basis for continuous tracking of how, when, where, and to what degree materiality is "becoming."[21]

Other studies also are beginning to indicate how current technology can track evolutions in what is becoming material and relate those changes to other data trends. And to do so in near to real time. Serafeim et al. "...studied whether during the 2020 COVID-19 induced market crash, investors differentiate across companies based on a firm's human capital, supply chain and operating crisis response [finding that] that companies with more positive [SASB based ESG] sentiment exhibit higher institutional investor money flows and less negative returns than their competitors." The period under study was extremely short (just over four weeks in February and March 2020) but is indicative of what could be called explosive materiality. Explosive materiality occurs in a rapid paradigm shift. The pandemic was clearly exceptional, but it was, for this purpose, highly illustrative of an exponentially accelerated process of "becoming material;" some factors which were immaterial or less intensively material prior to the event became extraordinarily material as the social context around them changed. For instance, the study found statistically strong correlations between the social measurements of human capital and supply chain resilience and strong relative equity performance (in a dramatically down market), as well as statistically significant higher inflows of institutional capital during the early months of the pandemic.[22] "Explosive materiality" might be the closest that real-world conditions ever get to the idealized context of MPT, in that there is an explosion of information, the information is rapidly disseminated and analyzed, the Values to value dynamic is sped up, and materiality for previously ignored factors is achieved in a very short period of time. That is far from a validation of MPT in the real world, however. First, and most obviously, a theory that works only in extremes is more thought experiment than universally applicable. In some ways, it is reminiscent of Coase's embrace of unfettered markets... except in the majority of cases where real world conditions make such an embrace uncomfortable and inefficient. Second, the TVL data used in the Serafeim et al. study was near real time and preceded the price movements. And it reflected pre-existing conditions at the companies that were not yet "material" in terms of impact on price before the pandemic's effects were manifest. So, even in the situation of "explosive materiality," the limitations of MPT taking into account non-price leading indicators through the efficient dissemination and absorption of information is demonstrated, although admittedly minimized in terms of time lag.

The Covid-19 pandemic provided a real-world, real-time context to test new data-gathering methods, which illustrated the idea of "becoming material" in a rapidly accelerated instance, demonstrating "dynamic materiality." Another study found that the volume of relevant news in five Covid-19 specific categories exploded from just over 10 percent of all news ingested at the onset of the pandemic in Europe and the USA in late January 2020 to almost 60 percent by the third week of March. The specifics of the explosion of new categories stakeholders appeared to consider material varied by industry and sector but affected the entire economy. None of these categories was taken to be material across that many sectors and industries prior to the pandemic. The explosion of this often-new material factors took place within about four weeks. As Tom Kuh noted in the Truvalue Labs study, it is suggestive of where big data analytics is able to take the materiality discussion.[23]

These recent studies share a more complex and nuanced, empirically based view of the process of becoming material. In this vein, a paper by Consolandi, Eccles, and Gabbi developed the idea of materiality intensity. They focused on what they termed the financial intensity of materiality, which they defined as the ratio between the number of material issues by industry sector for a company, compared with the total number of potential issues, whether material to that sector or not. They also analyzed what they term the financial relevance of materiality, which is the ratio between the value drivers impacted by a specific material issue and the 13 value drivers identified by SASB. From these two calculations, they develop a more nuanced view of what materiality means and how to analyze it, as well as what the market rewards (as measured by equity premia). The researchers went beyond the binary, static question of "material or not," instead focusing on the "financial relevance and intensity of ESG materiality."[24] They find that only a combination of both financial relevance of materiality and intensity of materiality have statistically significant results when looking for equity premia. They conclude: "For investors, our results show that when they consider ESG momentum [of ESG factors] they also need to focus on the concentration of material issue as one of the criteria for portfolio management. The market does not believe that having too many material targets is credible. Better fewer, but better."[25]

It might be that we are on the cusp of redefining what materiality is – and of what becoming material is – at least insofar as the market is concerned. (As discussed earlier, legal definitions often follow market consensus, albeit not always and not in any consistent time frame.)

Portfolio and System-Level Materiality

If MPT fails to consider how things become material, the opposite is also true: Definitions of materiality do not consider how the world invests today, which is in a manner consistent with MPT's portfolio focus. Legally, in the USA, materiality relates to what facts a reasonable investor would consider in making an investment in a particular security. As we shall see, much of the rest of the world, particularly Europe, considers societal or stakeholder informational needs, as well as those of investors, through an emerging "double materiality" standard. However, under either paradigm, materiality relates to facts about, or disclosures by, a company or other entity. Yet the essence of MPT is that it is the overall investment portfolio that matters, not the performance of any one security from any one issuer. As investors focus more on systematic risk as a driver of returns, their focus continues to broaden beyond compartmentalized information about individual companies. To be sure, disclosure by issuers and facts about securities are needed, but there is also information that a reasonable investor would like to know in making its investment decision which relates to the health of the environmental, social, and financial systems and the impact of the conditions of those systems on its portfolio, for, as we have seen with the explosive materiality example stemming from the Covid-19 pandemic, those systems can seriously and suddenly impact the portfolio risk/return profile. As part of the information necessary to judge developments affecting systemic health, an investor focusing on a portfolio, rather than an individual security, might reasonably be expected to be interested in various companies' impacts on those systems. However, an individual company is not likely to be attuned to, or want to bear the costs of, disclosures that are material to an investors' portfolio of investments but not as impactful to that individual issuer's securities. The European Union's (EU) new "double materiality" standard (see below) comes close but fails to actually create measures of system health. This is the disclosure/materiality equivalent of the MPT paradox; we have created materiality as a concept around individual securities, even though systems-related issues have more impact on the total return of a portfolio. Externalities, whether positive or negative, are exactly that for any one company – external. They might or might not be material for an investment decision vis-à-vis that company's securities. Simply put, materiality has a tragedy of the commons, or more pointedly, tragedy of the portfolio, problem; by defining materiality vis-à-vis a specific security, current definitions actually make it harder for a diversified investor attuned to the power of systematic risk to assess the relevant facts that drive portfolio risk and return.

Double Materiality

As at the time of writing, the most significant rethinking of the Values to value dynamic and redefinition of materiality is taking place in the EU. Focused on that region's societal norm shifts towards mitigating climate risk, the process of becoming material has moved far beyond portions of the market adopting "green" thinking and is now firmly in the process of becoming codified. The goal is to make the EU carbon neutral by 2050, in order to align with the 2016 Paris Climate Agreement. There are a number of elements to the European Green Deal and the Action Plan for Sustainable Finance, and, as at the time of writing, both are very much moving targets. But our goal here is not to fully discuss or describe them but rather to examine how norm and political shifts affect regulation, standardization, and disclosure, and how this impacts definitions of materiality as an important stage in the Values to value process.

The Green Deal and Action Plan are the broad umbrellas for a number of EU work streams, e.g. sustainable finance, taxonomy of environmental standards and categories, a green bond standard, climate benchmarks and disclosure. For example, the Climate Taxonomy focused initially on climate adaptation and carbon mitigation, both of which require standardized highly specific and technical disclosure by firms. These provide the data for financial firms' portfolio composition required in order to label a product "green," thereby attempting to minimize or eliminate greenwashing.[26] The Taxonomy is a dictionary; neither a set of mandated standards, an investment list nor an exclusion list, but an attempt to have comparable standards for companies and for financial institutions' products in order to incentivize environmentally sustainable activities.[27] Clearly, the Green Deal and Action Plan will have a global impact for standard setting dynamics and for firms' environmental (and social) standardized disclosure.

The EU's actions reflect and codify norm shifts; political and social movements. Many of these issues are systemic (e.g. climate, biodiversity, institutional health resiliency since Covid-19), which give rise to non-diversifiable systematic risks to a portfolio. However, these regulatory trends and actions will redefine market risk (beta) from the outside, which is complementary to (and partly caused by) actions by some financial market participants themselves as they attempt to change the market's risk profile (make beta better), for example, through corporate governance engagement and proxy voting, through public policy pressures by various investors (see chapter 5). The limitations of MPT, efficient markets, and instantaneous information absorption are brought into high focus by the EU's need to define materiality as "double materiality."

In 2019 the EU published a supplement updating earlier recommendations providing firms guidance consistent with the Task Force on Climate-Related Disclosure and the Non-Financial Reporting Directive of the EU.[28] The supplement states that the Reporting Directive, "…has a double materiality perspective." The first part is relevant to investors, although more broadly defined than what might appear in mandated financial accounting disclosures. Regarding climate, it states that relevant information, "…should be reported if it is necessary for an understanding of the development, performance and position of the company." This, the first part of double materiality is, in accord with SASB's view, in effect how climate factors impact a company. It is the outside-in view.

However, the second element of materiality is the inside-out perspective, disclosing how a company's external impacts affect "…citizens, consumers, employees, communities and civil society organizations…[because] an increasing number of investors also need to know about the climate impacts of investee companies in order to better understand and measure the climate impacts of their investment portfolios." Thus, in the non-binding words of the Directive, "Companies should consider using the proposed disclosures…if they decide that climate is a material issue from either of these two perspectives."

The double materiality idea is captured in Figure 4.1:[29]

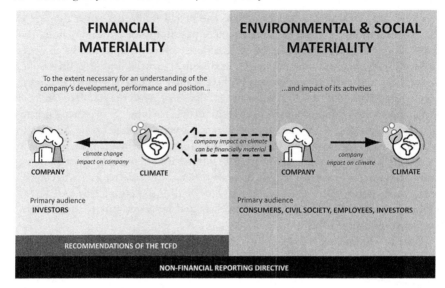

Figure 4.1 Double Materiality
Source: EU consultation document on the update of the non-binding guidelines on non-financial reporting

Revealingly, the Directive states that these two sides of materiality are "likely to overlap...[a]s markets and public policies evolve in response to climate change, the positive and/or negative impacts of a company on the climate will increasingly translate into business opportunities and/or risk that are financial material."[30] In effect, then, double materiality appears to be a forceable grafting of traditional investor view relating to financial relevance and a stakeholder view (although its definition of stakeholders is very broad) focused on impact: What does a firm do to society, what are its impact(s) on specific social sectors, regions, etc.[31] But these seemingly clear divisions glide over and minimize the actual dynamics of the relation between the two. While the Directive's "likely to overlap" statement suggests an important element, one that directly relates to the Values and value "becoming material" dynamic, the relation between investors and other stakeholders is more than an overlap. Rather, it suggests a moving symbiosis: Two different types of "beings" in a mutual relation with one another, sometimes beneficial, sometimes conflicting, never static. The important factor here are the feedback loops and structural integration (as discussed in chapter 1) of large, dominant investors into the broad economy, and its dependence on "society." Stakeholders and shareholders/share owners are not demarcated entities or lines in the sand, but rather a complex spectra of institutions, individuals, and interests.

In some ways, this is the twenty-first-century, institutionalized version of Adam Smith's being able to see self-interest and sympathy for fellow human beings as complementary, not antithetical. However, Smith, although writing

250 years before the EU was founded, was more advanced in one way: He understood that a single individual could encompass both "inside-out" and "outside-in" motivations, whereas the EU seems to think that investors are always investors, and non-investor stakeholders are always non-investor stakeholders, and never-the-twain-shall meet. The reality, especially today, is much more complex. As discussed in chapter 1, the structural changes in the market, particularly the institutionalization of asset management, means that most asset managers and even most asset owners, are fiduciaries for savers whose capital has been intermediated. Those savers are stakeholders as well. Moreover, the asset managers and asset owners are increasingly likely to be universal owners, whose concern with portfolio companies' externalities (the inside-out version of materiality) is likely to be at least partly because they understand that such externalities will affect the environmental, social, and financial systems on which the health of their overall portfolios rely. So, the inside-out impacts become outside-in, for the very same investors. This bridges the alleged gap or even juxtaposition between stakeholders and stockowners/stockholders.

A conceptualization of "singularity" materiality as dynamic and emerging, if focused on universal (and increasingly often other) investors and owners, contains both the outside-in and the inside-out (externality) elements. This is not to disparage in the least the important and critical issues of concern either to civil society or to investors, nor to deny that the EU's double materiality concept is a great improvement over the USA's very limited outside-in evaluation related to a single security (rather than a portfolio) but rather to underscore the complexity of the Values to value dynamic of materiality.

Extended Risk/Extended Intermediation

While the bifurcation of inside-out and outside-in materiality is, in some ways a simplification of how individuals and institutions actually relate to information, it does have advantages. It is a great improvement over limited financial information related to a single company or security being the definition of material, as it makes the Values to value dynamic explicit. It also parallels the twin purposes of finance. As postulated in chapter 2, finance is, or normatively should be, a service function. Specifically, asset management provides risk mitigation/return generation for investors (outside in materiality) and allocates capital where it is needed by the real economy (inside-out materiality). While this also oversimplifies the relationship between the purposes, understanding purpose immediately negates the common refrain of profit in and of itself as asset management's rationale for existence. "Making money" is not a purpose for the asset management industry, but a necessary condition, much like breathing is required for living, but is not the purpose of life. Profit should of course not be underestimated. Life would stop without breath; profit rewards the asset management industry and allows its perpetuation. Absent profit, the industry would cease to exist and thus risk mitigation and intermediation would stop. But it is an error to confuse an essential input into self-perpetuation for the industry with the industry's broader socio-economic purpose.

In this broader purpose-focused framework, we suggest that the question of time frame is absent from much of the discussion. We have already seen how the Values to value dynamic changes over time. For asset management to be sustainable (as a business, as well as in the other senses of the word) the twin functions need to be fulfilled not just in terms of how well the system performs risk/return optimization and intermediation currently, but also how well those current decisions affect the future risk/return profile and allocation of capital. Inter-temporal conflict means that decisions that seem to make sense today can result in an untenable tomorrow. Or a more beneficial one.

Even without considering the distant future, the risk mitigation/return function is neither simple to understand nor to execute. Risk is multi-dimensional, and minimizing one risk can increase another. For example, permanent loss of capital is among many people's worst fears. Somebody can easily mitigate that risk by keeping investments in cash, but that subjects them to inflation risk. Such an action also affects intermediation, as cash is usually tied to bank or bank-like institutions, meaning that the capital available intermediation and economic growth will be debt or loan-like, not equity. The complex relationship between investors seeking the appropriate level of risk and return – and intermediation – is ever present.

Current risk mitigation, at least on a relative basis, is what MPT excels at: Creating the best monetary return possible per unit of risk (defined as volatility) through the math of diversification. This is also true in the broader and more developed MPT tradition. Even with multiple factor investment strategies, or highly focused factor portfolios, the goal is still return per unit(s) of risk. Yet these are a necessary but entirely insufficient aspect of risk mitigation: Witness the financial crisis of 2008 where diversification was, at best, relatively ineffective at mitigating risk, and, at worst, contributed to the systemic breakdown, because diversification takes the market as it is, and tries to extract the most risk-efficient portfolio from it, even when that least variable portfolio is, by any definition, risky. But there is another dimension of risk management that MPT misses. Risk management should be multi-temporal, as well as multi-dimensional. In a nutshell, what we mean by this is that risk mitigation certainly needs to concern itself with the financial return to the investor per unit of risk (and, as we have argued, vis–à-vis the total return, not just relative return, which implies a concern for systemic health), but also the conditions in which the financial return can be expended.

Traditional financial risk assessment focuses entirely on current monetary returns. But that return, like so much of the MPT tradition, is sealed away from reality. In this case, those returns are disconnected from conditions of life. This means the broader context in which future income flows (the results from invest-ing) are expected to be expended. A retirement pension disbursal to an individual will obviously be spent in the context of the conditions in which that individual lives during his or her retirement years. For instance, from a traditional financial point of view, long periods of inflation or deflation different than what was anticipated would, looked at *ex post* from some future date, change the judgment about how effectively risk/return decisions were made years before. From a conditions of life point of view, if climate change or pollution impacts the health and welfare (or asset values, e.g. home ownership) of the individual, even an extremely good financial return will probably not buy the conditions of life that might have existed when savings and investment began. Or if social unrest created by increased levels of income inequality force somebody to live in a gated community surrounded by security guards and electrified fences like some dystopian science fiction movie (or to live outside such a community looking in), the financial return might not be adequate compensation for the inability to live in a socially cohesive environment. To put it somewhat more technically, there is not a market clearing discount value calculation for conditions of life to enable one to price future conditions of life. By discount value, we mean the ability to normalize future cash flows so that they are equivalent to current cash flows in terms of utility to the individual, in principle a net present value (NPV) conceptualization that takes the individual's personal utility value into account, or, more broadly, the utility value of the changed conditions of life as they affect society as a whole. Were such a discount rate to be conceived, it would vary widely according to the perceptions of the people whose lives will be affected in different ways. Utility values are notoriously hard to calculate among different people. But the lack of mathematical precision vis-à-vis an NPV calculation does not negate the direct and immediate connection between future conditions of life (as a risk factor) and today's financial markets.

This is another input into the "becoming material" feedback loop. As dystopian or utopian, or even just different, visions of future states become accepted as more or less probable, the factors that promote or retard them are considered more or less material. As an example, as the idea of global warming became more understood and accepted, individuals began thinking of greenhouse gas (GHG) emissions as material because they increasingly thought about extended risk mitigation. In other words, it is not so much that the incremental discharge of GHG would affect risk/return of a specific company today, but that it would change the conditions of life tomorrow. The fact that we do not have a discount rate on which everyone agrees for such a future does not and should not stop the market – or society, or EU regulators – from considering it material.

While extended risk mitigation might at first appear to be simply another way to think about the Values to value evolution towards materiality (i.e. most people do not want to live in a future world that is so hot that biodiversity is challenged, sea levels flood coastal cities, and human health is affected, so those Values become material), it actually differs from the Values to value dynamic in one key aspect. Extended risk mitigation analysis admits, as uncomfortable as it might be, that there are some whose decisions on such matters depends not on Values or "moral sentiments," but on value as well. That is, although putting discount rate on future conditions of life cannot be done for all, individuals use heuristics to implicitly calculate how much current financial reward they would accept in return for those future conditions of life. Thus, some people might be willing to accept a globally warmed world in return for financial return today. Looked at from extended risk viewpoint, the analysis becomes a tri-part mathematical problem, although the quantification of it is difficult and often impossible. Are those people willing to accept global warming willing to do so because: 1) They question the probable future state (e.g. climate change deniers as opposed to those worried about climate change) and/or the science which states that human action is the cause of the probable future state; or 2) Do they currently receive a pecuniary reward that they think compensates them for the future conditions of life (e.g. cheap energy); or 3) Are they just putting a different discount rate on the future state than the majority of the population concerned about climate change?

The second purpose of asset management, intermediation, relies on aggregation of savers' and investors' assets to redeploy those assets in a productive way into the real economy. We also note, in passing, that intermediation in practice overlaps with risk mitigation, as the aggregation aspect allows for greater risk spreading than an individual or small groups of individuals could do on their own. Theoretically, aggregation is not necessary for intermediation, but, in practice, it is an aspect of the vast majority of intermediated assets.

As with risk mitigation, however, the horizons of intermediation need to be extended. The difference is that the extension is both temporal and horizontal; that is, the extended view includes intermediation's effect on systems as well on the providers of capital and ultimate users of that capital, over time.

Today's state of intermediation – with tens of agents standing between savers and their investments – sometimes alienates savers from their rights and responsibilities as providers of capital. Considering extended intermediation is a way to minimize that alienation, while considering conditions of life over time. Concretely this suggests an additional focus on the efficient allocation of capital for the economy and society. A critical component of extended intermediation analysis is how asset management accounts for (or too typically does not account for) the costs (or benefits) of economic externalities. A positive or negative externality is an effect on a party that did not choose to incur either the cost or benefit of a contract, process, product, or service. For example, when an industrial plant discharges insufficiently treated wastewater into a river, downstream users of water feel the effects, but have not been a participant in the decision chain that caused the discharge. Such external costs can be either pecuniary or non-pecuniary, the former having a clear monetary impact (the cost of making polluted water cleaner at the moment) or non-pecuniary (the loss of enjoyment of a riverine landscape). (Of course, externalities can also be positive. For instance, in the hypothetical example that was suggested, increased economic activity around the industrial plant could provide money for schools, which would then increase both education levels and land values in the community.) For either pecuniary or non-pecuniary externalities, the long-term impact is real. To the degree that asset markets, owners, and managers ignore externality effects of their investments, the intermediation process is less than optimal. Traditional notions of intermediation do not capture this idea.

For example, carbon emissions over time affect the value of various assets (e.g. home prices; agricultural land) both positively and negatively, depending on location. They also affect some costs (e.g. weather-related insurance coverage). There are additional direct and indirect effects both pecuniary and non-pecuniary (e.g. weather-related refugee migration, loss of species), or, as we term it, the conditions of life. These are examples of the close relation between risk and intermediation impact on prices, valuations, and financial markets.

In order not to violate the core meaning of sustainability ("...development that meets the needs of the present without compromising the ability of future generations to meet their own needs."[32]), factoring in extended risk and extended intermediation should be an element in all asset management investment decisions and processes. Extended intermediation takes account not only of the financial processes, but also the consequences of the intermediation process itself: How the intermediation process alienates (or not) the ultimate providers of capital from the users of that capital. For example, an individual who invests in a FTSE 100 tracker (a passive index) is a partial owner of major British companies. Yet the intermediation process – investing through an advisor, who buys a tracker, created by an asset management firm, etc. – divorces capital from ownership. This is parallel to Berle's and Means' classical formulation of the divorce of ownership and control in the individual firm. Indeed, corporate ownership and institutional ownership divorces intersect in a host of ways that Berle and Means did not foresee. As a result, few investors understand that such investment is actually fractional ownership. Indeed, the performative results of MPT – the growth in index funds and the institutionalization of asset management – have meant that large asset managers such as State Street, BlackRock, Legal & General, and others – have become material agents of those fractional owners, voting with their shares and affecting corporate governance. That is not necessarily bad (they could be more equipped to perform such ownership responsibilities than the average retail investor), but it is a result of extended intermediation, which was not envisioned as an eventual result when MPT was proposed nor by the MPT ecosystem that has followed. Finally, the concept of extended intermediation implies that there is also extended disintermediation. Traditional disintermediation occurs when the chain of agents between a saver and his/her investment being put to productive use is reduced. For example, a person might invest in an equity directly through a dividend reinvestment plan, thereby disintermediating a bank or a broker. Extended disintermediation, however, also considers what the impact of not making an investment is on society. So, for example, one study found that only 1 percent of the capital allocated to 10,000 entrepreneurs by venture capital funds in the USA went to Black businesspeople. Women received only 9 percent of the funding.[33] As with extended intermediation, there are societal aspects to consider with extended disintermediation. Sometimes, those aspects can be positive, as when disintermediation of agents in the investment chain increases the linkage between investors and their governance rights or makes economic transactions more efficient. But sometimes they can be negative, as when racial or gender discrimination creates barriers to efficient allocation of capital. That, in turn, can exacerbate income inequality between groups with limited access to capital and those with such access, which can create social tensions and social and economic barriers to widespread adoption of new techniques to improve economic welfare overall or a more unequal economic benefit which affects social cohesion and conditions of life. This has been an issue for centuries, from the Luddites – who were middle-class weavers in the UK in the early nineteenth century, confronted by the Industrial Revolution, whose revolt against machines taking their jobs led to violence,[34] and then to the Dickensian working conditions of the early Industrial Revolution – to the digital divide today.

Everything old is new again. "Becoming Material," "Dual Materiality," "Extended Risk Mitigation," and "Extended Intermediation" are new concepts, but they reflect classical economic concerns about how finance and the real world interact. In that way, they reject the artificiality of the MPT tradition's limiting investment theory to hermetically sealed math, which "works" because the capital markets are assumed to be efficient at all times, humans are assumed to be calculating machines acting only out of self-interest, and neither institutions nor theory matter. Smith, Coase, Marx, Williamson, and even Friedman debunked those notions, but somehow the MPT tradition has managed to ignore those criticisms. To be sure, understanding the world's impact on our investments, and our investments' impact on the world, is not easy. Becoming material, dual materiality, extended risk, and extended intermediation are not as "elegant" as MPT in their analyses, because the real world is complex and sometimes downright messy. But it is ours; we live in it. Unlike MPT, these concepts build on the challenge from Smith, Coase, Marx, Williamson, and Friedman: To at least try.

Notes

1 Adam Smith. *The Theory of Moral Sentiments*. (1759, revised 1790), chapter III, first paragraph, at: www.econlib.org/library/Smith/smMS.html?chapter_num=2#book-reader (1790 ed.).
2 Ibid, sixth paragraph (np).
3 Ibid, part 2, section 2, chapter 3.
4 Ibid, part VI, section I; conclusion of the sixth part.
5 Ronald H. Coase. "The Problem of Social Costs," *The Journal of Law and Economics* (Vol. III, October 1960). For Coase's qualifications regarding transaction costs and the more general limiting assumptions see pp. 10, 15–16. Oliver E. Williamson, "The New Institutional Economics: Taking Stock, Looking Ahead," *Journal of Economic Literature* (XXXVII), September 2000, p. 599.
6 Coase. Ibid, p. 43.
7 Williamson, *Op cit.*, p. 595.
8 Williamson, "Transaction cost economics and organizational theory," originally in, *Industry and Corporate Change*, 1993, p. 89, at: www.researchgate.net/profile/Oliver_Williamson3/publication/31462357_Transaction_Cost_Economics_and_Organization_Theory/links/5655fd8c08ae1ef92979be1e.pdf.
9 Williamson. 'Transaction cost economics', chapter 3, p. 44, at: https://studfile.net/preview/5714480/page:5; and Williamson, *Op.cit.* (2000), p. 602. See also "Transaction

cost economics: an introduction" (2007), p. 3, at: www.econstor.eu/bitstream/10419/17926/1/dp2007-3.pdf

10 Ibid. (2007), p. 5.

11 Milton Friedman. "The social responsibility of the business is to increase profits," September 13, 1970, at: http://umich.edu/~thecore/doc/Friedman.pdf.

12 Adolph Berle and Gardiner Means. *The Modern Corporation and Private Property* (New York: 1932).

13 Friedman. *Op. cit.*

14 Duncan Austin. "Pigou and the Dropped Stitch of Economics," February 2020, at: https://preventablesurprises.com/wp-content/uploads/2020/02/Pigou-and-The-Dropped-Stitch-of-Economics.pdf.

15 *Contribution to the Critique of Hegel's Philosophy of Right*, 1843–44, at: www.marxists.org/archive/marx/works/1844/df-jahrbucher/law-abs.htm.

16 See Robert G. Eccles and Tim Youmans. "Materiality in Corporate Governance: The Statement of Significant Audiences and Materiality." Harvard Business School Working Paper, No. 16–023, September 2015. They discuss "significant audiences" of materiality (stakeholders) and how and why boards of firms should and legally are able to take these voices into account, in addition to shareowners. See also Jean Rogers and George Serafeim. "Pathway to Materiality: How sustainability issues become financial material to corporations and their investors," Harvard Business School Working Paper 20–056, 2019.

17 Lisa Penaloza and Alladi Vankatesh. "Further evolving the new dominant logic of marketing: from services to the social construction of markets," *Marketing Theory* (August 2006, 6(3); and Karl Polanyi. *The Great Transformation* (1944).

18 Truvalue Labs. "Dynamic Materiality: Measuring what matters" (2019), at: https://insights.truvaluelabs.com/white-paper/dynamic-materiality-download.

19 Serafeim and Rogers. *Op. cit.* p. 4.

20 "Embracing the New Age of Materiality; Harnessing the pace of change in ESG," World Economic Forum (in collaboration with Boston Consulting Group), March 2020, pp. 7–10.

21 Truvalue Labs. *Op. cit.*

22 "Corporate resilience and Response during COVID-19," Alex Cheema-Fox, Bridget R. LaPerla, George Serafeim, and Hui (Stacie) Wang, June 23, 2020, p. 7. Available at: https://papers.ssrn.com/sol3/papers.cfm?abstract_id=3578167. Quotation is from an earlier draft of April 17 2020.

23 Tom Kuh. "ESG After CCOVID-19: Will it be different this time?", April 2020, p. 2, available at: www.truvaluelabs.com/blog/esg-after-covid-19-will-it-be-different-this-time; a version also at: www.ipe.com/viewpoint-esg-after-covid-19-will-it-be-different-this-time/10046023.article.

24 Costanza Consolandi, Robert G. Eccles, and Giampaolo Gabbi. "Better Few but Belter: stock returns and the financial relevance and financial of materiality," April 2020. pp. 3–4. Available at: https://papers.ssrn.com/sol3/papers.cfm?abstract_id=3574547.

25 Ibid., p. 22. Their measure of centration is the Gini index.

26 European Commission. "Sustainable Finance," at: https://ec.europa.eu/info/business-economy-euro/banking-and-finance/sustainable-finance_en.

27 There has been significant criticism of the taxonomy from a number of angles. Ben Caldecott of Oxford University summarizes some of these in *Responsible Investor* in a brief articled titled: [the Taxonomy] "'Encourages laziness and disincentives ambition': Ben Caldecott shares his thoughts on the EU's green taxonomy," at: www.responsible-investor.com/articles/encourages-laziness-and-disincentives-ambition-ben-caldecott-shares-his-tho. See also: Stan Duprè The EU's Risky Green Taxonomy, at: www.project-syndicate.org/commentary/european-union-green-taxonomy-three-questions-by-stan-dupre-2020-01?barrier=accesspaylog.

28 Consultation document on the update of the non-binding guidelines on non-financial reporting, at: https://ec.europa.eu/info/sites/info/files/business_economy_euro/banking_a nd_finance/documents/2019-non-financial-reporting-guidelines-consultation-document_ en.pdf. (nd) We note that the widespread use of the term "non-financial," in this document but far more widespread, is entirely confusing and misplaced. If something is material in any dimension financially then it must be material. How could something relevant, in a broad or technical sense, to value creation and valuation be "non-financial" yet material? A better term for emerging E and S and G issues is "not-yet-financial," meaning not yet broadly accepted by market participants and/or regulatory authorities; something emerging. This process is also captured, as discussed, by Truvalue Labs' idea of dynamic materiality and by the World Economic Forum's term emerging materiality.

29 Ibid. pp. 7–8.

30 Ibid. p. 7. Disclosures while not mandated (pre-2020 taxonomy) also did not have specific standards or metrics, but the guidelines stated that firms should look to disclosure frameworks of the Global Reporting Initiative, the CDP (formerly Carbon Disclosure Project), the Carbon Disclosure Standards Board, SASB, and the International Integrated Reporting Council.

31 See Cristiano Busco, Costanza Consolandi, Robert G. Eccles and Elena Sofra. "A preliminary Analysis of SASB Reporting: Disclosure Topics, Financial Relevance, and the Financial Intensity of ESG Materiality," *Journal of Applied Corporate Finance*, Vol. 32, issue 2, 2020, at: https://papers.ssrn.com/sol3/papers.cfm?abstract_ id=3548849.

32 www.iisd.org/topic/sustainable-development. Accessed August 23, 2017.

33 Mary Ann Azevedo. "Untapped Opportunity: Minority Founders Still Being Overlooked." *Crunchbase News*, February 27, 2019. At: https://news.crunchbase.com/ news/untapped-opportunity-minority-founders-still-being-overlooked. Accessed August 15, 2020.

34 Clive Thompson. "When Robots Take all our Jobs Remember the Luddites", Smithsonian Magazine, January, 2017. At www.smithsonianmag.com/innovation/when-robots-take-jobs-remember-luddites-180961423. Accessed August 15, 2020.

5   From Dividends in Nutmeg to Creating $5 Trillion
Welcome to the Third Stage of Corporate Governance

Stage three corporate governance and its signature feature – investors attempting to mitigate systematic risks – did not happen overnight. It took four centuries to get here.

Stage Zero: Nutmeg. Then 350 Years of Stasis

The history of the corporation and of corporate governance begins with the formation of the first modern corporation, the Dutch East India Company (in Dutch, the Verenigde Oost-Indische Compagnie, VOC), in 1602.[1] The VOC's turbulent existence foreshadowed the big issues that would become headlines centuries later. How they were resolved set many of the fault lines for modern corporate governance:

- Executive compensation. Contemporary Dutch commentators noted that insiders grew their fortunes quickly and without much transparency, "in the manner of mushrooms."[2]
- Shareowner versus stakeholder controversy. The question of the purpose of the VOC loomed large in its history. Was it an instrumentality of the state, designed to increase Dutch trade and influence in Asia, or should it serve the shareholders who had invested?[3]
- Capital structure and an appropriate return to shareholders. Isaac Le Maire, the world's first shareholder activist, complained that the VOC did not make any dividend payments. His petition read, in part "It is indefensible that a company board could, under whatever pretext, retain another's money for longer or use it in ways other than the latter wishes, for that would be a type of tyranny."[4] Soon thereafter the VOC did pay a dividend, but later it began to pay in pepper and nutmeg, rather than in money.[5]
- Power. In the end, Le Maire, despite being an extremely wealthy merchant, was overmatched by the corporate power of the VOC. As one modern-day academic concluded: "Le Maire's impassioned plea for the rights of VOC shareholders was rebuffed. The odds were stacked against him inasmuch as the state authorities to whom he was appealing had an interest in reaffirming the very power Le Maire was challenging, an explanation that resonates quite loudly today."[6]

It is remarkable how little changed for more than three-and-a-half centuries — and how much has changed in the past three decades.

Perhaps that explains why Harry Markowitz, writing exactly 350 years after the VOC's founding, completely ignored the corporate governance issues that exploded into modern finance consciousness a few decades later: The idea of investors actually being able to influence real world value creation or mitigate risk seemed as futile in 1952 as it did in LeMaire's time. Markowitz was reflecting the world he knew; the only world that had existed since the age of European exploration. No wonder the Modern Portfolio Theory (MPT) tradition is a self-referential system, sealed away from the real economy, and using only price — whether in nutmeg or dollars — as the metric of value realized, with no regard as to how that value actually is created or destroyed or whether it can be enhanced, because, as Berle and Means had written 20 years before Markowitz, the separation of ownership and management led to the managers being able to effectively dominate, leaving owners at risk and with little ability to enhance or even influence value creation. They were allowed only "the wages of capital," namely dividends and stock price.[7] In some ways, price, as the summary metric of value creation for MPT, is the equivalent of volatility as the summary metric of how risk is created. Both measure the result, rather than provide any visibility into the value or risk creation process or how to improve the result. That omission highlights the limitations of the MPT tradition.

The 350-year period of stasis, from the founding of the VOC until the last half of the twentieth century, is the pre-history of the modern corporate governance movement. Call it "stage zero," as it forms the foundation from which stages one, two, and three governance evolved. It is the starting point for the path dependent history of why investors, corporations, regulators, executives, and boards act as they do.

Of course, over the course of three-and-a-half centuries, some specific facts and situations changed. Empires rose and fell. Jurisdictions created different corporate laws. Royal or national charters stopped being tailored specifically for each company. The limited duration of the charters expanded and eventually became open-ended. Corporations became common as a form of commercial enterprise, despite some well-known skeptics, such as Adam Smith, the father of economics, who famously wrote: "To establish a joint stock company, for any undertaking, merely because such a company might be capable of managing it successfully... would certainly not be reasonable.... The directors being managers of other people's money than their own, it cannot be well expected that they would watch over it with... anxious vigilance... Negligence and profusion, therefore, must always prevail, more or less, in the management of the affairs of such a company."[8]

What did not change was that corporate executives continued to be, if not imperial, then at least the locus of power in the corporate ecosystem. (There is, of course, one entity with the power to check corporate executives, which is government. Historically, it has shown intermittent and contradictory desires to rein in or unleash corporations, depending on political expediency. As with the

VOC, governments often count on corporations to do their bidding, and, in some jurisdictions, corporate lobbying and campaign contributions help to determine the political environment and government's desire or diffidence to be a counterweight. Whatever the political environment, however, within corporations, executives – principally CEOs – reigned supreme.)

Even the nominal governors of the corporation – the directors – were subservient to the executives well into, and largely throughout, the twentieth century. In 1973, following a study of US corporate Boards of Directors, Harvard Business School Professor Myles Mace called them "ornaments on a corporate Christmas tree."[9] Peter Drucker, an influential management academic of the second half of the twentieth century, agreed. Even as late as 1993, he noted that: "There is one thing all boards have in common. They do not function."[10]

That began to change right around the time that Drucker wrote those words, but it was still common enough. Managerial power had been ingrained for so long that even as the twenty-first century dawned, some CEOs continued to enjoy a sense of entitlement, with the goal of running "their" company with as little "interference" as possible. In 2002 one of this book's co-authors (Lukomnik) was on the creditors' committee that ultimately rehabilitated Worldcom, a giant telecom company. Worldcom was, at the time, the subject of the largest corporate fraud and bankruptcy in the history of the world. He was a member of the committee tasked with finding a new CEO and recalls interviewing one particular candidate. The candidate was asked for his view on corporate governance for Worldcom, going forward. Would he have an independent Chair of the Board? An independent nominating committee? How would he empower the board? Remember, this was a company in bankruptcy as a result of massive fraud. It even had former SEC Chairman Richard C. Breeden as a court-appointed special examiner to oversee it. Yet the candidate's answer reflected the 350 years of managerial power and the culture that it had created, not the fact-specific needs of the company. The candidate's answer was "I'll be damned if I have someone looking over my shoulder as I run my company." The candidate was not selected. (He later went on to run a different Fortune 500 company, which he did poorly.)

Under the surface, however, power was shifting. Most importantly, the capital markets were rapidly institutionalizing, and, as noted in chapter 1, MPT was at least partly the cause. In the USA, for example, mutual funds, which pre-packaged diversification, were on the rise. Between 1960 until 1965 assets in mutual funds doubled. Then, from 1965 until 1970 they doubled again.[11] Legislative passage of the Employee Retirement Income Security Act (ERISA) of 1974 and the creation of tax-advantaged 401k retirement accounts four years later served both as validation of the importance of pension investing and turbocharged the growth in assets. The aggregate result of MPT, ERISA, and other factors is that the ratio of retail to institutional holdings in the US equity market changed from less than 8 percent institutional and 92 percent retail in 1950 (two years before Markowitz's paper)[12], to institutional investors controlling nearly 40 percent of the equity market in 1981,[13] to more than 80 percent institutional by 2017.[14] It is worth stating the obvious: Power in a capitalist society depends on who controls the capital. The ability of corporations to access permanent capital at a scale unreachable for investors had, for 350 years, determined the power relationship between the corporations and investors. With institutional investors now having as much, or more capital than corporations, the power dynamic between companies and investors was changing.[15] Similar power changes were occurring in the European Union (EU), the UK, Australia, and other jurisdictions. While each jurisdiction had its idiosyncrasies, the directionality – the rise of a professional class of investing intermediaries with ever increasing amounts of capital – was nearly universal.

Stage One: From "Negligence and Profusion" Comes Change

However, while institutional investors might have been amassing capital, they had not yet demonstrated the ability, or even the willingness, to use it. To be sure, there had been attempts to use investor power to impact Values, but not value directly, at least not on a widespread basis. The most muscular movement – against apartheid in South Africa – was firmly based in the Socially Responsible Investor movement, although it did attract some others, notably a few public pension funds and other large asset owners that were beginning to understand universal ownership issues. But those causes – although important precursors which gave experience to a generation of corporate governance activists – never blossomed into a more widespread commitment to use all that newly amassed capital as fuel to create value more generally. Ultimately, the sparks that ignited the corporate governance awakening were, as Smith had warned, caused by the "negligence and profusion" of some corporate managers.

The combination of institutionalization of assets and negligence and profusion shaped the corporate governance landscape of the 1980s stock market in the USA into something out of a science fiction novel or fantasy universe. It featured "greenmail" and "dead-hand poison pills." It was populated by "raiders" and "white knights." Fights used strategies entitled "Pacman defenses" and "good-bye kisses." If those phrases suggest an environment wherein upstarts battled against long-established power, that was what, in fact, was happening.

The proximate cause of the birth of the modern corporate governance movement was greenmail. Greenmail, now largely outlawed or otherwise proscribed, was the 1980s capital market equivalent of a cyber-ransom attack. A raider bought stock in a company and then threatened the long-settled and comfortable life of the CEO and the Board with a hostile take-over. Instead of asking for payment through a cryptocurrency transfer, the raider asked the CEO to buy back the raider's shares, at a premium to the market. Which the companies did. Over and over and over.

Greenmail was everywhere in the early 1980s. David Murdock, a director who dared to confront legendarily imperial Occidental Petroleum CEO Armand Hammer, was paid $194 million for his shares, at a 42 percent premium to the market, in return for going away, in a "good-bye kiss."[16] Sir James Goldsmith rolled over the Goodyear Tire and Rubber Company for $93 million.[17] Saul

Steinberg extracted $47 million from Quaker State Oil Refining Company (which paid him $24 a share on a day that the stock closed at $16.13),[18] and then another $60 million from The Walt Disney Company.[19] In one year, ended April 1984, greenmail cost US corporations, or, more precisely, the shareowners of US corporations, some $4 billion.[20] Those numbers are not adjusted for inflation.

The raiders were happy – and rich. The CEOs and Directors were happy – and still in charge. But the shareholders, whose money was used for those ransom payments, were incensed. In the old days, as Le Maire discovered, that would have been irrelevant. But this time, when shareowners decided to fight back, they were somewhat successful. Welcome to stage one of corporate governance.

Steinberg's raid on Walt Disney made an impression on one institutional asset owner in particular: Jesse Unruh, the legendary "Big Daddy" of California politics in the 1970s and 1980s. Unruh tipped the scales at nearly 300 pounds. But his Big Daddy nickname did not just refer to his girth. It also highlighted his skill at wielding money and power. By the mid-1980s he had a great deal of both. Unruh was California's Treasurer, a state-wide elected position that made him a board member of both the California Public Employees Retirement System (CalPERS) and the California State Teachers Retirement System (CalSTRS), the largest two pension funds in the USA.

The Disney payment to Steinberg infuriated Unruh. Unlike earlier conflicts such as South Africa or pharmaceutical companies marketing infant formula to emerging market mothers who could not afford it, there was no arguing about Values or value. The transfer of value to greenmailers by rent-seeking corporate executives was clearly center-stage and in the spotlight. The market reaction to the payment to Steinberg slashed the market value of Disney by half a billion dollars and cost the two California pension funds $7.5 million. "There must be some better way than sitting by and getting ripped off," Unruh said.[21] He found it. Together with his counterparts in New York City[22] and New Jersey, he established the Council of Institutional Investors. Initially formed by 21 pension funds with the aggregate total of assets under management of some $100 billion, it was an extension of Unruh's personality: Smart, political, combative when it needed to be, comforting at other times. But most of all, it knew how to combine money, power, and political savvy. (Today, CII is still the leading voice of investor-led governance in the US, comprised of 135 asset owner members, with some $4 trillion in assets. CII also has more than 60 large asset managers as associate members, with more than $35 trillion in assets under management.[23] Clearly, Unruh recognized a need.)

At first, CII played defense, focusing on abuses like greenmail. To protect their economic interests, CII members tried to change the structures and processes which enabled such rent-seeking actions by corporate insiders. CII issued a Shareholder's Bill of Rights that called for equal treatment of all shareholders. The very idea of shareholders objecting to corporate management was so revolutionary that the *The Washington Post* article on the shareholder bill of rights began:

"Kings of corporate management beware: Your once loyal and passive subjects have declared their independence by adopting the Shareholder Bill of Rights. No longer will your biggest stockholders stand idly by as you take away their right to vote on questions as crucial as who will rule the corporate kingdom. Gone are the days when shareholders will watch silently as top executives adopt antitakeover devices that entrench management and depress stock prices."[24]

CII leveraged the few points in corporate law where investors had power, such as merger and acquisition battles and changes to capital structure. A fight over an oil company recapitalization drew bold-faced names like T. Boone Pickens, Carl Icahn, and Ivan Boesky (soon to be convicted of insider trading) to duke it out. This was reality television before reality television. The plot line was simple: Billions of dollars at stake, and powerful people confronting other powerful people. It was standing room only in front of a forest of television cameras. Beneath the drama, however, it was clear that a new era was dawning. As Harrison J. Goldin, one of the co-Chairs of the Council said when the Bill of Rights was announced, "We have done something very important, even revolutionary... We are asserting the role of investors as a new force."[25] Le Maire could not have said it better. The difference was that CII had as much capital as did most corporations.

Of course, the power relationships among investors, directors, and executives did not change overnight. Even greenmail and good-bye kisses continued for some time. In 1986 Roger Smith, the CEO of industrial icon General Motors, kicked iconoclast businessman H. Ross Perot (and future independent Presidential candidate) off the board of GM. He also paid Perot $700 million for his shares and to go away. What had changed was the ability of even GM's CEO to do so without challenge. CII wrote to Smith, demanding a meeting. Smith initially refused. Goldin issued an ultimatum. "If this Chairman of GM won't meet with us," he said, "perhaps the next one will." Smith caved within days.[26]

"Do Better"

The defensive focus of stage one corporate governance began to change following a 1987 speech at a CII meeting by famed lawyer Ira Millstein, later one of the "wise men" who drafted the initial OECD principles of corporate governance. Milstein urged the investors to focus on the boards of directors at underperforming companies.[27] As he said, the ideal shareholder resolution would be exactly two words long: "do better."[28] This call for investors to engage with corporations was a direct assault on MPT's divorce of investing from real-world intervention. While few realized it at the time, Millstein ushered in not just a corporate governance revolution, but the primordial stage of investors working outside the parameters of MPT to increase returns and reduce risk. In a non-statistical sense, these actions created a new type of "efficient frontier," one that when successful actually could change in a statistical sense the parameters of MPT's efficient frontier.

Among those who heard Millstein's message loud and clear was Dale Hansen. Hansen had been appointed Executive Director of CalPERS, the largest pension fund in the USA, just weeks before hearing Millstein's call to arms. "It took a while to sink in, but that is what we eventually resolved to do," he said[29]. CalPERS soon reformed its corporate governance program to focus on underperformers, setting an example for virtually every other investor. It was, Hanson said, a way to "move the herd,"[30] as one herds cattle to move forward by focusing on the outliers, or as lions chase zebras, focusing on the slower ones.

Once performance became a selection criterion, people decided to measure performance. A study of companies on CalPERS' target list of underperformers found that those companies had underperformed the S&P 500 by more than 75 percent in the five years prior to CalPERS' intervention but outperformed by more than 50 percent in the five years following.[31] Shortly thereafter, McKinsey said that investors would pay 11 percent more for a well-governed company.[32] Those two contemporaneous studies helped to convince a critical mass of institutional asset owners, advisors, and the financial press that corporate governance could play both defense and offense. (There was much controversy over the quality of the Wilshire study, but successive studies seem to show persistence. In 2013 Wilshire re-examined the CalPERS study and found the cumulative excess five-year return averaged 13.7% above the Russell 1000 index and 12.1% when corrected for industry sectors.[33])

Both the CalPERS target list study and the McKinsey study amplified Millstein's suggestion that investors had a role to play in the real world, as well as in capital markets. If there were an 11 percent discount that could be closed by real-world intervention; then why limit investing to trading? Why not try to close that discount and reap some of the premium? Investors began to move from price takers on the trading floor to influencing price through board room dynamics. The barrier between what MPT considered investing – security selection and portfolio construction – and what CalPERS and others considered investing, which added real-world interventions – was breaking down. Practice transcended existing MPT theory and opened the way for a new investing paradigm.

Similar developments were happening across the Atlantic Ocean, and in one situation, actually in the Atlantic.

Sir Adrian Cadbury was one of the most respected British. businessmen of the late twentieth and early twenty-first centuries, not only because of his stewardship of the eponymous candy company, but for his huge impact on corporate governance globally. When he agreed in 1991 to chair an all-star commission examining "The Financial Aspects of Corporate Governance," British textile company Polly Peck had already collapsed and contributed to the context for the review. But that was a minor scandal compared with what would occur next. On November 5, 1991, Robert Maxwell, the UK's dominant media baron and power broker, was found missing from his yacht off the coast of the Canary Islands.[34] It emerged that Maxwell had pilfered billions of pounds from the corporate pension funds to try to prop up various unprofitable businesses.[35] Soon his empire was in complete disarray.

"When our Committee was formed just over eighteen months ago, neither our title nor our work programme seemed framed to catch the headlines... the continuing concern about standards of financial reporting and accountability, heightened by BCCI[36], Maxwell and the controversy over directors' pay, which have kept corporate governance in the public eye," Sir Adrian wrote in the preface to the 1992 report.[37] "Unexpected though this attention may have been, it reflects a climate of opinion which accepts that changes are needed and it presents an opportunity to raise standards of which we should take full advantage."[38]

Take advantage he did. In what came to be known as the Cadbury code, the report outlined a "Code of Best Practice" for British companies. It was the first widely adopted corporate governance code, and became hugely influential not just in the UK, but around the world. In a nice instance of symmetry, Cadbury joined Millstein in 1998 as two of the six authors of a report from the Business Sector Advisory Group to the OECD, "Corporate Governance: Improving Competitiveness and Access to Capital in Global Markets" which set the stage for the OECD's own 1999 code.[39]

Soon codes of corporate governance were being adopted globally. Today, only three OECD countries (the USA, China, and India) do not have such codes.[40] These were, to be sure, codes for companies, not investors. But the codes were designed as "comply or explain,"[41] and the explanation was to the capital markets. The new role of investors was to hold companies to account.

Hermes, a British asset manager, took that responsibility seriously. The Hermes Principles, published in 2002, were the first widely recognized code designed by, and for, investors. Even the cover of the report made that clear; it featured the following: "What shareholders expect of public companies – and what companies should expect of their investors."[42] Placing explicit responsibilities upon investors was not the only innovation. The Hermes code explicitly took on the time frame discussion and argued that the companies should focus on value creation over the long term, rather than yield to short-term market pressures. It specifically discussed corporate obligations to stakeholders other than shareholders (Principle 9) and that companies should "minimize the externalization of costs to the detriment of society" (Principle 10).[43]

Stage one corporate governance largely remained on individual company governance. The now popular acronym, ESG, for environmental, social and governance factors, had not yet been born. It was not that the E&S of ESG were ignored, as the Hermes Principles made clear. Indeed, many of the leaders of stage one corporate governance had earlier, formative experiences in E&S battles. New York City's Goldin, for example, traced his involvement in corporate governance to the mid-1970s efforts around trying to get pharmaceutical companies to act ethically and to stop weaning poor women in developing countries off breast-feeding their infants in order to sell them baby formula. He had later been involved in a comprehensive anti-apartheid effort to get companies to either leave South Africa, or, at the least, stop supplying the apartheid government with tools to enforce its racist policies.[44]

Indeed, what soon emerged as a core stage one corporate governance tactic – using shareholder proposals at annual meetings – stemmed from an "S" issue: The South Africa apartheid battle. Peter Clapman, then general counsel at TIAA-CREF, a major US asset manager specializing in providing services to colleges and universities, was a veteran of the South Africa apartheid battles. Clapman was the first to suggest using shareholder resolutions, which had been a staple of the South African campaign, for governance issues.[45]

As to the "E", the CERES Principles, a set of environmental principles, were developed with Goldin's office by Joan Bavaria, the president of Franklin Research and Development, one of the first dedicated Socially Responsible Investors (Franklin later became Trillium Asset Management).[46] In 1989 the Exxon oil tanker *Valdez* crashed in Prince William Sound in Alaska, besmirching what had been wilderness and sending television images of dying, oil-covered sea birds and aquatic mammals around the world.[47] The spill cost Exxon about $15 billion in market value.[48] Environmentalists and investors alike were convinced that "environmental issues were deferred contingent liabilities, able to explode suddenly and rip holes in balance sheets much as the Bligh Reef had ripped open the hull of the *Valdez*." [49]

The CERES Principles were initially called the Valdez principles, until one of the early participating companies objected. When CERES asked Ben & Jerry's Ice Cream to become a signatory, the company suggested changing the name, noting that calling the statement the "Valdez Principles" was like "naming Audubon the dead oily bird society."[50] Today, CERES is a leading sustainability non-government organization (NGO), working with the world's biggest investors and corporations. CERES is also an incubator of other organizations. The Global Reporting Initiative grew out of CERES.[51]

Stage 2: Redefining Value

The focus through the first decades of increased shareholder power was firmly on governance, with E&S usually playing a supporting role and only occasionally grabbing the center-stage spotlight. That changed in 2005, when then UN Secretary-General Kofi Annan invited 20 large institutional investors to design what would become the Principles for Responsible Investment (PRI).[52]

This is stage two corporate governance, with the E and S as equal co-stars to the G. The purpose of modern corporate governance remained the performance of firms and of their capital market securities. But stage two governance broadened the definition of performance from a somewhat narrow, purely financial statement performance focus, to a more macro-economic view. In that way, it more closely aligned with universal owner theory and that theory's view of externalities being reincorporated into large investors' portfolios. It also aligned with the desire of investors to begin addressing the systemic risks that can affect market volatility through feedback loops from the real economy to the capital markets, and vice-versa. Finally, it also anticipated today's increasing acceptance that sustainable profitability results from corporations solving societal problems, rather than exploiting them.

While corporate governance is much more than shareholder resolutions or votes, those data points are illuminative. In 2019 in the USA, there were 457 environmental or social resolutions filed with companies for votes at their annual general meetings, up from about 400 at the beginning of the decade, ranging from reporting on climate change to human capital management issues. Average support on these resolutions has increased by 40 percent in the last decade, from about 18 percent in 2010 to nearly 26 percent in 2019,[53] reflecting the increasing awareness that a healthy real-world society and economy are prerequisites to healthy capital markets.

Stage two corporate governance expanded the focus from a narrow definition on financial performance and "traditional" corporate governance concerns (that is, traditional from the mid-1980s) to include environmental and social concerns. But the focus remained on individual companies. To the extent that there was any attempt to address systematic or systemic risks, the tactics reached back to the Dale Hanson era goal of getting the herd to run. But investors were still doing that by targeting slow cattle. They did not give the herd vitamins.

However, among some of the largest institutions in the world, the realization that the economy and society was what mattered, rather than any individual investment, was starting to percolate. By 2010, Martin Skancke, the Norwegian Ministry of Finance official in charge of its sovereign wealth fund, would write: "The Fund has a very long investment horizon. The nature of the Fund's diversified portfolio has been referred to as universal ownership. When most economic activity impacts your portfolio (negatively or positively) on the margin, there is no rationale to support exploitive behavior in any one portfolio company. This is the essential difference between the Fund and the average investor."[54]

Understanding that difference, that the health of the economy rather than that of "any one portfolio company" was what really mattered, set the stage for stage three corporate governance.

Stage 3: Focusing on Systematic Risks

Though it builds on stages one and two and incorporates them, third stage corporate governance differs in that it targets systematic risks, not individual companies or securities. In that sense, stage three corporate governance activities to mitigate systematic risks can be layered atop MPT's use of diversification to mitigate idiosyncratic risks. Of course, to change the risk/return profile of the market requires understanding and then somehow affecting the causes of systematic risk and return. That, in turn, expands the definition of materiality, as discussed in chapter 4, to those issues which affect the financial, social, and environmental systems. In effect, we are back to Smith, Karl Marx, Ronald Coase, Oliver Williamson, and Milton Friedman and their direct and indirect acknowledgement of the feedback loops between the real-world and economic decision-making, including those decisions which determine market dynamics.

Perhaps the purest example of third stage governance's perspective came from the world's largest asset owner. In November 2017 Hiromichi Mizuno, the

Executive Managing Director of the Japanese Government Pension Investment Fund (GPIF), with assets of about $1.4 trillion, noted that, owing to its sheer size, its returns are overwhelmingly a function of the real-world economy, rather than of beating a benchmark. Understanding the limitations of the MPT paradox, he said that seeking alpha was largely irrelevant to the fund (less than a rounding error) and then announced that GPIF would hire specialty investment managers to focus on environmental and social concerns, in an effort to impact society and the economy. The G of ESG was not ignored; GPIF already had a Governance program that was run internally.[55]

This type of beta activism is not limited to asset owners. In the UK, Legal & General Investment Management (LGIM), the asset management portion of Legal & General, is well known for its stewardship activities. As of February 2020 LGIM had assets under management of about $1.5 trillion and was the fourth largest index manager in the world. LGIM notes that "we strive to achieve positive societal impacts, in the belief that it will create more sustainable long-term value," which is classic stage two macro performance theory. But it also says that it will try to influence not only company, but also market behavior (emphasis added) in various ways, including "influencing governments, regulators and policy makers" and by "collaborating with other investors and stakeholders," which moves it to stage three behavior. Here is a page from its website:[56]

> At LGIM we take our stewardship responsibilities seriously and devote significant resource to ensure our clients' assets are protected and enhanced over time.
>
> **We take an active and impactful approach to stewardship by using our scale as a global investment manager to influence and change company and market behaviors. In doing so, we strive to achieve positive societal impacts, in the belief that it will create more sustainable long-term value.**
>
> We do this through:
>
> Company engagement
> Using our voting rights globally
> Integrating environmental, social and governance factors into portfolio management
> Addressing systemic risks and opportunities
> Influencing governments, regulators and policy makers
> Collaborating with other investors and stakeholders

It is worth noting that LGIM's definition of investing includes: Influencing regulators, policymakers, NGOs, and other investors, as well as companies; jawboning the market; educating its clients as to how to mitigate systematic risk in investing; and private sector standard-setting, for instance by announcing that it will vote against any combined chair/CEO board members in order to urge the separation of the two roles.[57]

This is typical of stage three governance investors who move beyond trading securities for relative return on an electronic terminal to use what The Investment Integration Project (TIIP) calls the "tools of intentionality" to affect capital markets and total market return by affecting the systems on which capital markets rely. TIIP notes that the key differentiating points of investors who consider system level thinking is that they act with intentionality. TIIP identifies ten such activities. As we shall see, investors are using all of them, and more. While one could quibble with the details of TIIP's taxonomy, intentionality is clearly present in all those third stage governance activities.

It is not an accident that GPIF and LGIM each have more than $1 trillion dollars in assets under management. As Martin Skancke noted about Norway's sovereign wealth fund, they have nowhere to hide from market risk and therefore have adopted some aspects of universal owner thinking. Universal owners, whether or not they self-identify as such, intuitively (and increasingly explicitly) understand that they will be exposed to market risk and market returns for long periods and are too large to expect much of their return to come from non-marketwide systematic risk. Some come to realize that they can try to affect the real-world systemic risks that in turn cause markets to become more or less risk-averse. An additional benefit of their size is that it makes them more likely to successfully impact those real-world conditions (although as we will see later, small firms can be successful through creative use of multiple tools of intentionality). LGIM, for instance, caused a stir in 2020 when it announced its campaign against chairpersons who also served as CEOs.[58] Yet dividing the Chair and CEO roles has been an issue among corporate governance cognoscenti for more than a decade.[59] LGIM's position received attention precisely because it was large and because it announced that it would vote against Board directors at companies that continued to combine the roles.

"We Are All Universal Owners Now"

Many smaller institutions, and even retail investors, today regard themselves as universal owners, caring about the systems on which the capital markets depend. Partly, that is due to the growth in indexing: If you accept that your returns will be those of the market, then you should care about the health of the overall market (rather than that of the securities that you have selected). Others intuitively believe that a healthy capital market relies on a healthy economy and society. Others are motivated by a desire for social responsibility and, in effect, the ideas of extended risk and extended intermediation (See chapter 4). Ellen Quigley of Cambridge University's Centre for Study of Existential Risk says simply that investors today have no choice but to think about systematic (and, given her institute's focus, systemic) risk. "We are all universal owners now," she concludes.[60]

Quigley argues that large universal owners in particular, by using governance and policy engagement in addition to various investment strategies, are "material devices." By being early first movers capable of influencing basic norm

The Ten Tools of Intentionality: Defined

These tools — described below — represent specific pathways through which investors can bridge the gap between daily portfolio management decision-making and systems-level investing. Investors use these tools intentionally because the portfolio-level discipline of efficiency alone does not naturally lead them to do so. Through each of these ten tools, investors manifest their concerns about risks and rewards at systems levels and facilitate impact in a variety of ways.

 Additionality is the intentional decision to pursue investments that provide access to finance to the underserved and address unmet environmental or social needs. Through this approach, investors seek to enhance the resilience and stability of overarching environmental, societal, and financial systems by addressing social inequalities and social and environmental market failures and, in doing so, increase opportunities for the investment market.

 Diversity of Approach is the intentional decision to utilize a diverse range of investment tools to address complex systems-level environmental and social concerns. For asset owners this means adopting a broad variety of approaches to addressing single systems-level considerations. For asset managers it means creating multiple investment options for clients concerned with the systems relevant to their investment objectives, increasing investors' influence on complex systems through multiplicity of initiatives.

 Evaluations is the intentional decision to value the difficult-to-price aspects of environmental, societal and financial systems that generate potential long-term wealth creation, societal and environmental value, and investment opportunities. Using this approach, investors think beyond quantifiable price and evaluate the potential of these aspects of systems to provide the stability and predictability necessary to create a fertile field of such opportunities.

 Interconnectedness is the intentional effort by investors to increase the flow of information and communications about environmental, societal and financial systems among peers and with clients and the public at large. Through Interconnectedness, investors not only seek to increase the amount, but also the effectiveness of these information flows on systems. In doing so, this approach recognizes the importance of having a shared knowledge base to manage common-pooled sources of wealth creation and in avoiding a "tragedy of the commons."

 Locality is the intentional decision to make investments that strengthen the environmental or societal systems within a given geographic area—be that a city, state, region or country. Such investments can simultaneously generate economic growth within a region and enhance its resilience and sustainability through support of interrelated enterprises. This approach seeks competitive short-term returns that also build a foundation for future investment opportunities in the long term.

 Polity is the intentional engagement by investors in public policy debates with the goal of creating stronger, more resilient financial, environmental or societal systems. This approach seeks to use the rules and regulations established by government to effectively enhance the environmental social and financial systems creating a rising tide for all investors and devising market mechanisms that facilitate investors' ability to positively impact these systems.

Figure 5.1a and 5.1b The ten TIIP tools of intentionality
Courtesy of The Investment Integration Project. Used with permission.

Self-Organization is the intentional decision by investors to create on-going organizational structures that build the capacity of the investment community to address systems-related considerations and strengthen the overall resilience of the financial system. This approach seeks to assist the industry in the development of its members, individually and collectively, to effectively influence the systems within which they operate.

Solutions is the intentional decision to pursue investments that can solve societal and environmental challenges in ways that support the stability and enhancement of environmental, societal and financial systems. This approach seeks to identify investment opportunities that not only profit from the most pressing systems-level challenges of the day but also that resolve them positively. A Solutions approach can fundamentally alter the nature of systems, creating versions of these systems with more positive dynamics and more extensive investment opportunities.

Standards Setting is the intentional decision by investors to establish standards that discourage investments in corporations, industries and countries with practices that violate broadly accepted standards or norms, or to contribute to the development of such standards. This approach aims to avoid crises of trust in the financial community that can arise when its members take actions that undercut societal, environmental or financial systems-level norms. At the same time, it seeks to lend legitimacy to financial institutions through the implementation of higher standards. In doing so these standards can help strengthen the overall systems themselves and assure their long-term viability as a source of wealth creation.

Utility is the intentional decision to maximize the alignment of the specific investments within a portfolio's asset classes with the societal functions that these asset classes were designed to serve. This approach assumes that the characteristics of, and market for, each asset class differ because they serve distinct societal functions. For example, investors use public equities to actively participate in various ways in sharing in the private wealth generated by large corporations; fixed income typically provides low-risk opportunities to allocate assets to a range of government initiatives that create those public goods not easily served by private markets; venture capital allows high-risk investments in disruptive products and services; and so on. Utility seeks to enhance the effective functioning of asset classes within the overall financial system—a system that depends on a diversity of differently structured financial products to serve a variety of social and environmental needs.

Figure 5.1a and 5.1b (Cont.)

shifts, they become a "norm entrepreneur."[61] Using climate change as an example, she explains that "Evolutions in social norms often reflect, and are reflected by, changes in the law. The concept of fiduciary duty – especially as it relates to responsible investment – has undergone significant changes over the last few decades. Incorporating climate risk into an institutions' investment decisions was first prohibited, then permitted, and may soon become mandatory. In some jurisdictions divestment or exclusions were only thought to be allowed if they had no negative affect on financial performance, and indeed many funds have cited fiduciary duty as a reason for not divesting from fossil fuels. Divestment and exclusions are now widely permitted, however, and there are hints that factoring climate risk into investments may become mandatory. This evolution has tracked society's growing concern over climate change."[62]

The idea that universal owners influence smaller investors, retail ones included, to consider climate change as a risk to their investments is a direct challenge to the MPT tradition. Of course, the focus on the cause of risk, rather than on volatility, challenges MPT by directly connecting the investment portfolio dots to the broadly socioeconomic ones. Put a bit differently, it would mean that investors are considering that systemic climate risk manifests in their portfolios as systematic risk, and that, potentially, continuing to hold those securities contributes to that increased volatility of betas. The investors are then faced with a choice: Continuing to invest in fossil fuel investments might, at any individual moment, result in a "better" risk/return profile in terms of mean variance, but it potentially threatens and devalues other sectors of the portfolio. Therefore, understanding the impacts of the choice to continue to invest in fossil fuel-related assets in terms of risk/return demands a reconceptualization of maximizing risk/return in a way that includes both traditional MPT-type diversification, but also consideration of the impact of the portfolio itself for ongoing systematic risk. Indeed, we note that all investments have intermediation/allocation of capital impacts not accounted for by MPT. The fossil fuel example is valuable because the implications are widely speculated upon. We also note that various forms of investment might have more or less intermediation impact. For example, divesting from a company's stock in the secondary market, particularly if done quietly, might not have as much impact as refusing to buy a new bond of the same company and making that announcement publicly. In the first instance, there is no impact (or at most only an indirect one) on the company's capital base and little signal to the market of the investor's concerns that might encourage similar action. In the second, there is a direct impact on the company's cost of capital and new information provided to the market highlighting an investor's concerns.

That might explain the explosion in all types of investors undertaking beta activism activities, across a range of systematic risks. Even so, we note a type of schizophrenia, wherein investors say that they believe in the basic precepts of MPT, such as efficient markets, yet take action against systematic risk in a way that belies their words. They seem to suffer from a pseudo-Stockholm syndrome, wherein they mimic the words of their intellectual captor – in this case MPT – even while they secretly (if not unconsciously) yearn for freedom from MPT's assertion of helplessness against systematic risk and impotence in affecting total market return. As just one example, consider the case of Allianz. The co-authors of this book presented some of the ideas contained herein – and particularly the idea of "better beta," in a 2018 white paper published by the Pension Insurance Corporation (PIC)[63] As part of that project, PIC solicited reactions from the asset management industry, policymakers, academics, and others. Most were supportive, but the CEO of Allianz Global Investors voiced a full-throated MPT-based thumb-down. "The idea that one can improve 'beta returns' is the most fanciful of all. Directing capital towards certain sectors /activities... will likely lead to lower beta returns... as capital is 'wasted' from an efficient capital market perspective," he wrote.[64] Yet two months later, Allianz's parent company announced that it was 1) ceasing underwriting of coal-fired power plants and coal mines; 2) divesting from coal in its proprietary investments (albeit over a 20-year period); and 3) joining the science-based target initiatives collaboration to drive towards a carbon-free economy.[65]

Clearly, practice is leading, and sometimes denying, theory.

Combining Beta Activism and the MPT Tradition

In the contemporaneous instant, third stage governance activities are largely orthogonal to MPT's security selection and portfolio construction activities. Therefore, beta activism can be layered atop such traditional investing activities.

There is one exception to that statistical independence at the moment of use: Exclusions (divestitures) are perhaps the most controversial tool in the third stage corporate governance handbook specifically because they clearly affect MPT-based portfolio construction. The MPT argument is that by reducing the opportunity set from which the least mean variance portfolio can be constructed, the result is poorer diversification and, therefore, a greater variance.

The reality is quite a bit more complex. There are at least three foundational assumptions behind the idea that reducing the opportunity set reduces portfolio efficiency. The first is that the reduction in opportunity set actually impacts the ability to diversify in reality. The second assumption is that the securities excluded from consideration have characteristics that would positively impact the efficiency of the portfolio construction and that by removing them you decrease that efficiency. The third assumption is that the portfolio manager is skilled and will therefore select securities that combine to maximize the risk/ return of the portfolio, so a larger opportunity set is better.

Let's examine all three assumptions. The father of MPT himself, Markowitz, suggests that, in most cases, the reduction in the opportunity set created by such exclusions is virtually undetectable insofar as the benefits of diversification are concerned. Markowitz notes that the power of diversification falls as the number of non-correlated securities held in a portfolio increases. "(I)t seems safe to say that an ethics screen which reduced available securities from about 8,000 to about 4,000 would have to be quite strange to make it impossible to select a reasonably liquid, well diversified portfolio with returns comparable to those usually finds in portfolio of well-established companies with similar levels of portfolio volatility. ...(I)ndeed, efficient portfolios from the 4,000+ names of the ethically screened universe lose little in efficiency as compared to those from the full, 8,000+ name universe."[66]

However, we note that many exclusionary screens focus on a non-random set of securities (e.g. fossil fuel companies). In other words, exclusionary screens tend to remove a sector, or, in effect, a systematic risk factor. This makes the diminished value of marginal diversification argument less powerful, though still relevant. But it increases the relevance of the next assumption, that a larger opportunity set *ipso facto* means a better risk/return profile. Removing a high-risk/low-performing sector would improve the efficiency of the average portfolio. Exclusions are rarely random. They are made for a reason, and they are generally systematic risk reasons. For instance, an index provider might exclude securities with limited liquidity, as the rebalancing costs of using thinly traded securities will outweigh the increased efficiency of the resultant portfolio.[67] In such a case, exclusions are clearly designed to add to return. To use an "E" example, an investor might choose to exclude heavy carbon-footprint firms from a portfolio. If the systemic risk factor of carbon results in poorer performance over time, then the removal of those securities from the opportunity set will skew the remaining securities towards a more positive and probably more efficient risk/return profile. (However, if the systemic risk factor results in a positive bias, then the skew to the remaining securities would be negative.) In other words, the fact that exclusions are chosen for systematic risk factors means that they are systematically excluding securities whose price movements will largely correlate. From a high-level perspective this is a form of ESG-informed factor investing, and by definition selection/exclusion of factors reduces the investable universe. For instance, it is not controversial that a value investor would not invest in a high-price/earnings, high-price/book, high-price/revenue but high-growth company. Similarly, it should not be surprising that an investor concerned with carbon emissions should not want to invest in a high-emission company. To take a simple example, a value equity investor excludes growth stocks from the opportunity set for its portfolio. If, in fact, those securities are riskier or poorer performers, then the remaining opportunity set is improved, meaning that a portfolio manager is likely to benefit from having a more limited, but positively skewed, opportunity set.[68] As we pointed out in chapter 4 regarding dynamic or emerging materiality, exclusion of (or tilting for or against) a particular firm or sector also involves a necessary political judgment about stakeholders and regulators influence and power. To ignore these influences is willful blindness and undertaken at one's peril.

Finally, some portfolio managers are skilled, and some are not, and not all decisions are perfect, even when taken by skilled portfolio managers. Therefore, even if the excluded securities could be used to improve the optimization of the portfolio, or if the removals are random, there is no guarantee that the portfolio manager would have taken advantage of the larger opportunity set.

In sum, exclusions have fact-specific impacts. They do not always either improve or denigrate the risk-return profile of the resultant portfolio.[69] Unfortunately, there continues to be a powerful – but decaying – myth that considering Values automatically denigrates the risk/return profile of the resultant portfolio among some. In 2020 the US Department of Labor proposed a rule that would in effect discriminate against considering ESG factors in retirement investment funds. But that myth is believed by ever fewer people and by even fewer actual market participants. A total of 94 percent of the official comments submitted by the investment industry and others opposed the rule, and many pointed out that it was based on a fallacious assumption. (Only 2 percent supported it, and 4 percent were neutral.) It is safe to say that that would not have been the proportion 50 years ago.

Steve Lydenberg, the founder of TIIP and a veteran of responsible investing for more than 30 years, notes that exclusions represent a specific type of standard-setting tool and can occur for both "value" and "Values" reasons.[70] For example, a "Values" investor would choose a low-carbon footprint portfolio because of concerns about global warming. By contrast, a "value" investor might not care about global warming but could be concerned about regulatory risk or costs for high-carbon emitters or view a high-carbon business plan as evidence of corporate leadership failure. What is rarely contemplated, however, is the interplay between the value and Values investors, perhaps because it plays out over time in the real world, rather than instantaneously in the trading markets (see chapter 4). To use that same example, some "Values"-based investors have shunned the securities of heavy carbon-footprint companies for years. Perhaps they affect the cost of capital for heavy carbon-footprint companies, or perhaps they convince banks not to lend to new coal projects or insurers not to underwrite them, as Allianz decided. Moreover, those investors are also voters and members of society. They – and others – vote for governments to enact a regulatory regime that incentivizes a transition away from a carbon-based economy in many jurisdictions. Other consumers might boycott high carbon emitter firms (for example, by switching to alternative energy suppliers). As a result, a "value"-only investor might be cautious about including high carbon-footprint companies in its portfolio owing to business prospects, whatever its beliefs about global warming. As discussed, (chapter 4), if enough stakeholders (and stockowners and/or managers) believe in a given set of Values, this can affect value.

While exclusions (and positive inclusions) are the only third-stage corporate governance tool that is not orthogonal to MPT *at the moment of investment,* over time that statistical independence diminishes, owing largely to feedback mechanisms similar to the above. That makes sense: The premise of third stage corporate governance is that value and risk creation, which determine the MPT metrics of return, volatility, and correlation, occur in the real economy, so if investors want to increase systemic value and decrease systematic risk, they need to engage the systems that generate value and risk. There should, therefore, be feedback loops which will, in turn, affect expected correlations, volatilities, and returns.

We see two basic forms of such MPT/systems interactions over time. Perhaps the most obvious is that markets evolve to accommodate the creation of, or withdrawal of, products designed to achieve a third stage governance goal. Green bonds and low-carbon-impact index funds try to impact the environmental system, and social impact bonds and community finance development bonds exist to improve communities. Given the creativity of the financial sector, more and more such impact securities are sure to be created.[71] For example, investment banks have begun creating products that directly link financial terms to ESG goals. In 2020 Enel, an Italian-based energy company, issued a bond with the interest rate linked to the United Nations' Social Development Goals (SDG). If Enel achieves its SDG goals, the rate goes down. There is a step-up in interest rates if it does not. Three large Dutch pension plans were among the investors.[72] That is merely one example. According to Morgan Stanley, $32 billion of social and sustainability bonds were issued in April 2020, and that does not include green bonds. In fact, April 2020 was the first month in which social and sustainability bond issuance outpaced green bond issuance.[73] Such social-linked debt instruments are even making their way into bank loans: ING underwrites loans linked to a borrower's sustainability performance.[74] How long will it be until those loans are packages and securitized? Clearly, the risk/return of these instruments – and how they interact with an MPT portfolio – will not be orthogonal to MPT's security selection and portfolio construction activities over time.

More generally, as investors succeed in either sensitizing other investors to risks or opportunities, or affect real-world policy and practice, markets will rerate around the changed perceptions of those risks/opportunities, consistent with the theory of information adoption discussed in chapter 2.

We're All Beta Activists Now

What follows are six examples of beta activism around systematic risks. As the case study of the New York City pension funds' Boardroom Accessibility Project in chapter 2 focused on governance issues and because stewardship codes and other examples of third stage corporate governance activities are well known, we have chosen to include third stage governance campaigns focused on environmental and social system risks. This is far from a comprehensive list. Such an attempt would be foolhardy: Investors increasingly understand the feedback loops between capital markets, the economy, and society as a whole. Given that and given the ever-evolving nature of the environmental, social, and financial systems, new risks and opportunities are inevitable. (For example, climate change was not a concept until the second half of the twentieth century, and artificial intelligence was not advanced enough to pose systematic risk and opportunity until the first half of the twenty-first century.) We have selected these six and have attempted to highlight widely accepted systematic (and perhaps systemic) risks such as climate change and gender diversity, as well as emerging ones, such as antimicrobial resistance and artificial intelligence. The investors are diverse, from a smaller but thought-leading impact investor (Domini) to the largest investor in the world (BlackRock) and from a religious asset owner (Church of England) to a universal bank (Nordea). We apologize in advance for omitting innumerable other third stage investor initiatives that could easily have made this list. But these six, as well as the New York City Boardroom Accountability Project (BAP), are indicative of the scope and import of third stage corporate governance systematic risk mitigation/

opportunity enhancement efforts underway. Finally, we note that these brief synopses are meant as exemplars of the third stage governance approaches, rather than detailed case histories.

Climate Change

(Third stage governance tools used: Additionality, Diversity of Approach, Evaluations, Interconnectedness, Polity, Self-Organization, Solutions, Standard-Setting)

On January 11, 2020 Larry Fink, the CEO of BlackRock, told the world that "Climate Risk Is Investment Risk."[75] This was not news. Mark Carney, the Governor of the Bank of England, had been warning for years about a "Minsky Moment" when the values of carbon-related assets could collapse.[76] The Bank for International Settlement, which is the central bankers' central bank, had been saying for some time that central bankers cannot save the world's capital markets from climate risk, culminating a week after Fink's proclamation with its "Green Swan" report.[77] An investor coalition, partly organized by CERES, was instrumental in pushing through the Paris Climate Accords. There are billions and billions of dollars invested in low-carbon index funds and in clean-tech portfolios.

So, the pronouncement that "Climate Risk is Investment Risk" was not news. But the fact that BlackRock was saying it, made it the talk of the financial world. BlackRock is the world's largest asset management company, with some $7 trillion of assets under management. Fink has been writing letters to the CEOs of the portfolio companies in which BlackRock invests for many years. They have often focused on the need for companies to think long term and to have a societal purpose.

But BlackRock had been criticized by some for talking the talk, but not walking the walk, particularly when it comes to environmental issues. It had not, for example, joined Climate Action 100, a group of global investors dedicated to collective engagement with large carbon emitters, although 350 of its peers had. Some of its votes on shareholder resolutions relating to climate were inconsistent and, in the view of many climate activists, not helpful.[78] BlackRock explained this by saying that the votes were influenced by its private talks with companies. But those talks – and what was or was not accomplished by them – were not transparent.

BlackRock joined Climate Action 100 two days before Fink's letter.[79] Then, in his letter he wrote: "Climate change has become a defining factor in companies' long-term prospects.... I believe we are on the edge of a fundamental reshaping of finance... In the near future – and sooner than most anticipate – there will be a significant reallocation of capital." He went on to announce "a number of initiatives to place sustainability at the center of our investment approach, including: making sustainability integral to portfolio construction and risk management; exiting investments that present a high sustainability-related risk, such as thermal coal producers, launching new investment products that screen fossil fuels and strengthening our commitment to sustainability and transparency in our investment stewardship activities."

He then asked the CEOs to whom the letter was addressed to start reporting data according to Sustainability Accounting Standards Board (SASB) and Task Force on Climate-related Financial Disclosures (TCFD) standards. SASB is a foundation that has established a framework for "industry-specific disclosure standards across environmental, social, and governance topics." TCFD has suggested a set of "voluntary, consistent climate-related financial risk disclosures."[80]

Until Fink's request, reporting of ESG factors has been a ball of confusion, as governments and traditional accounting standard-setters have refused to regulate disclosure standards. The result is an alphabet soup of disclosure frameworks. SASB and TCFD to be sure, but also, in alphabetical order − CDP, EEI, GRESB, GRI, IIRC, IPIECA, and scores of others. A 2018 report noted that 78 percent of the S&P 500 companies issue sustainability reports, but that they had virtually no standardization. Ninety-seven percent of them customized their reports by picking and choosing from the various frameworks as they liked – one referenced six of those alphabet soup frameworks − or used no framework at all.[81] As a result there is little consistency or ability to compare companies' ESG efforts.

Fink's attempt at private sector standard-setting for ESG disclosure is definitely a stage three corporate governance tool. It promises to be game-changing.[82] Within days of Fink's letter going public, SASB saw an increase in inbound inquiries from corporations.

As noted, BlackRock was not a leader in the climate fight. Perhaps its position as the largest asset manager in the world meant that it could not move as quickly as others. But Fink's use of various tools of intentionality – standard-setting, additional products, interconnectedness – underscores that we are now in the third stage of modern corporate governance as much as it affirms that climate risk is investment risk.

Anti-microbial Resistance

(Third stage governance tools used: Evaluations, Interconnectedness, Locality, Polity, Standard-Setting)

As the Covid-19 pandemic that spread in early 2020 reminded the world, the linkage between global health and the economy is deep, wide, and persistent. Pandemics – from the plague to the global influenza pandemic of 1918–19 – have cruelly reshaped societies for millennia.

There were predictions of a coronavirus-based outbreak at least as far back as 2007. They were uncanny in their precision, even citing the suspected cause of the 2020 pandemic: the combination of coronaviruses in bats and the nature of Southern Chinese wet markets, where captive live mammals held in close proximity to each other are sold for human consumption.[83]

What might be the next global health threat to which we should be paying attention? One possibility is antimicrobial resistance (AMR) − the increasing ability of bacteria to evolve to become resistant to standard – and even some advanced – medical treatments. As former British Prime Minister David Cameron warned upon the release of a joint British and Wellcome Trust research review into AMR, "If we fail to act, we are looking at an almost unthinkable scenario where antibiotics no longer work and we are cast back into the dark ages of medicine."[84] Interestingly, the joint review was led by an economist, Jim O'Neill, best known for his work on emerging markets (he coined the phrase BRICs, for Brazil, Russia, India, China). As he wrote, "… tackling AMR… needs to be seen as the economic and security threat that it is."[85] The numbers are gob-smacking: Without intervention, AMR will cost 10 million lives and drain some $100 trillion from the global economy by 2050.[86] Drug-resistant bacteria are already blamed for 50,000 deaths a year in just Europe and the US.[87] This is the classic "preventable surprise," to use the phrase coined by positive investment maverick Raj Thamotheram.[88]

At least one investor, Nordea, is paying attention, and trying not to be taken by surprise. The largest Nordic banking group, Nordea manages about €325 billion.[89] It has undertaken a major effort in the pharmaceutical manufacturing sector in India. Together with China, India manufactures much of the world's medicine, including many antibiotics. However, that concentrated manufacturing sector has created both social and economic risks. Pharmaceutical ground water pollution facilitates the growth of antibiotic resistant microbes.

Upon visiting the manufacturing areas in India, Nordea "observed terrible water pollution, coming from the production of drugs supplied to the Western-based pharmaceutical industry…We took initiative to commission an independent on-the-ground investigation," writes Sasja Beslik.[90] The results of that investigation were presented to the Pharmaceutical Supply Chain Initiative, an industry association, and an action plan was put in place.[91] Less than four years later, in January 2020, the Indian government proposed new legislation limiting the amount of antibiotic effluent that can be released by pharmaceutical manufacturing facilities.[92]

Gender Diversity

(Third stage governance tools used: Additionality, Diversity of Approach, Evaluations, Interconnectedness, Solutions, Standard-Setting)

Visitors to Wall Street were surprised one morning in March 2017. Overnight, it seemed, "Fearless Girl" appeared. The young woman, cast in bronze, just four foot two inches high, with arms akimbo and hands on hips, defiantly staring into the space in front of her, was positioned to confront the iconic Wall Street bull sculpture. The press, public, and the industry were captivated immediately. Fearless Girl inspired television reports and t-shirts, internet memes, and essays.

She had been commissioned by State Street Global Advisors (SSGA), as part of its campaign to increase gender diversity in corporate boardrooms and executive suites.[93] State Street also publicized a number of studies showing the risks created by single gender boards of directors and then intervened with

Sculpture by Kristen Visbal, commissioned by State Street Global Advisors

Figure 5.2 Fearless Girl
Courtesy of State Street Global Advisors. Used with permission.

1,463 global companies that had all male boards, explicitly noting that single-gender boards were both sub-optimal and unacceptable. As at October 2020, 789 of the 11,483 had either added a female director or had pledged to do so.[94]

Gender diversity has been an issue for many other firms. The 30% Coalition was founded in 2011 to advocate for boardroom diversity and boasts investors with some $6 trillion in assets under management.[95] LGIM votes against the boards at all large British companies which have less than 25 percent female representation on their boards.[96] Both SSGA and LGIM have retail financial products that direct capital towards companies with high levels of gender diversity. This is an effort to address a systematic risk – lack of diversity – across the marketplace, not just at specific companies. This attempt at standard-setting by asset managers is working, if slowly. As recently as 2012, one in eight of the boards at S&P 500 companies were entirely male. By 2019 that number was zero.[97] Overall in US companies today, about 20 percent of directors are women; in the large cap S&P 500 companies that number increases to more than 27 percent.[98] The progress is slower than many would like, but the acceleration since asset managers and owners started focusing on gender diversity as a systematic issue, rather than an issue for specific companies, has been noticeable. Even the initial public offering market is starting to understand that gender diversity is the exception, not the rule. In 2019 only one major US corporation went public with an all-male board; in the three preceding years, about half had done so. Even Goldman Sachs, an exemplar of Wall Street power and often criticized for it, has made a major effort to improve gender – and racial – diversity. While CEO David Solomon's announcement that it will no longer serve as lead underwriter unless company's boards have at least one woman on them, with the number going to two in 2021,[99] received most of the attention, Goldman Sachs Asset Management also announced that it will vote against boards that are not gender diverse. Furthermore, more than half assets under management are managed by women,[100] "(H)aving a diverse team is as important as having a diverse mix of investments in the portfolio," noted GSAM Chairperson Sheila Patel. "When people look at the world differently, they find more solutions to problems and have a better shot at generating strong returns."

Research bears that out. A study by McKinsey in 2018 found that companies in the top quartile for gender diversity were 21 percent more likely to be more profitable than the industry median, and 27 percent more likely to create more value, than companies with bottom-quartile gender diversity performance.[101]

Deforestation

(Third stage governance tools used: Additionality, Diversity of Approach, Evaluations, Interconnectedness, Locality, Polity, Self-organization, Solutions, Standard-Setting, Utility)

Domini, a small New York-based asset manager, clearly embraces beta activism. It was founded by Amy Domini, a responsible investing pioneer, and has an outsized influence on other investors, largely because of its thought leadership. Recently, much of that thought leadership has focused on deforestation.

Domini takes an exceptionally deliberate approach to risk mitigation. The result uses all ten tools of intentionality and is a virtual how-to for investors seeking to have impact. Domini began its deforestation efforts by examining the economic, social, and environmental case for forests, noting that forests provide benefits such as clean air, food, a livelihood for various indigenous people, climate stability, and biodiversity. It then identified two root causes for deforestation – "short-term profit-taking... that extract(s) value from forests while undermining the long-term source of that value" and the lack of "an appropriate value and cost framework" and four proximate reasons: Demand for soy, beef, timber, and palm oil. We note that, although not universal to the systemic risks beta activists seek to mitigate, the lack of "an appropriate value and cost framework" is a common root cause to what beta activists see as a market failure. That is one reason that "Evaluations" or placing a value on difficult-to-quantify wealth- or risk- creators is one of TIIP's ten tools of intentionality.

After the causal research, Domini created a "forests belief statement to make explicit our understanding of the relevance of forests to our core investment practices and risk mitigation." Domini then developed forest effectiveness principles – a four-part statement that reads like a bullet-point version of third-stage corporate governance tactics.

1 Incorporate into our investments, engagements, and other operational decisions a holistic understanding of the corporate and investor dependence and impact on the long-term value and services from forests.
2 Work to create a positive system dynamic that enhances the value of forest systems.
3 Identify and monitor our direct and indirect impacts on forests considering both positive and negative effects.
4 Share our principles and process with investors, investees and the financial community to promote holistic, long-term policies and practices regarding forests.[102]

Domini also reviewed its internal key performance indicators for its forest project, resulting in 24 modifications, and mapped its forest efforts to the SDGs.[103] All that preparation resulted in a multi-faceted approach: Domini has invested in green bonds designed to protect forests in the USA and Brazil, proselytized with industry partners, created resources for other investors, worked with industry standard-setters such as the Roundtable for Sustainable Palm Oil (which later instituted a ban on deforestation), engaged with 79 companies, and Carol Laible, Domini's CEO, has spoken at industry events, elevating the firm's concerns to higher visibility.[104] Domini has also joined the Investor Initiative for Sustainable Forests – a joint initiative of CERES and the Principles for Responsible Investing.[105] The considered, holistic approach has given Domini outsized influence compared with what might be expected for a 26-person firm with just $2 billion in assets under management.[106] In early 2020 it led the 25-member, $440 billion investor coalition that supported the California Deforestation Free Procurement Act.[107] Indicative of Domini's foresight, the EU development of "taxonomies" on six "E" factors includes deforestation as a major issue about which there must be standardized disclosure after 2024.

Artificial Intelligence (AI)

(Third stage governance tools used: Interconnectedness, Polity, Self-Organization, Standard-Setting)

In January 2020 an automotive supply worker in Detroit was arrested by police for felony theft. It was a mistake. A bad facial recognition algorithm had identified an innocent man.[108] That incident is believed to be the first – but inevitably will not be the last – such case of wrongful arrest as a result of artificial intelligence (AI) bias.

That is worrying, not just for society but also for the economy and the capital markets. AI is rapidly colonizing virtually all aspects of business, from the auto sector's focus on self-driving cars, to the optimizations that drive social media, to finance's omnipresent algorithms. However, as it turns out, AI can be artificial stupidity. It can be wrong. It can even exhibit systematic bias. For example, facial recognition is more accurate for white people than for Black people and more accurate for men than women.[109] Shortly after the Detroit incident, worry that the artificial intelligence behind facial recognition had been poorly developed led Microsoft, Amazon, and IBM to cease, at least temporarily, sales of such products to the police.[110] It is not just racial bias: Allegations of faulty algorithms have suggested gender bias in extending credit at Goldman Sachs.[111] Such errors can be both illegal and costly. A British insurance company was fined £5.2 million for overreliance on poorly designed voice recognition software.[112] In addition to the fine, the insurance company abandoned the entire line of insurance that it had entered, which cost it multiples of the fine in lost opportunity cost.[113] Given the valuations given to new business models that use large amounts of data and AI – for example, Facebook and Alphabet – and the investment in applications of AI such as self-driving cars, drone delivery services, smart energy grids, and hundreds more, the potential disruptions to the economy and capital markets owing to bias or just plain sloppiness are both manifest and frightening.

Federated Hermes, a $600 billion asset manager,[114] has undertaken a standard-setting program, trying to combat three types of bias in AI – input data bias, process bias, and outcomes bias – in order to mitigate systematic risk from poor governance of AI, particularly in the financial sector.[115] The British-based asset manager contributed to two major reports on the issue and has created six principles for responsible AI use.[116] It has engaged with 60 portfolio companies in banking, technology, medical devices, and pharmaceuticals around the governance of AI risks. Federated Hermes also regularly participates in high-profile conferences with industry, regulators, and investors to bring attention to the issue.[117]

Investor Mining and Tailings Initiative

(Third stage governance tools used: Diversity of Approach, Interconnectedness, Locality, Polity, Standard-Setting)

Your cell phone contains mined materials. So does your car, your computer, your house, and virtually everything that you own. Investors are acutely aware that extractive industries are necessary for an economy increasingly driven by data, information, and technology. But those investors have reason to be concerned. While the products that come out of the mines might be inputs for the most current high technology available, and while the extractive industry certainly has updated many of its practices to twenty-first-century standards, some old economy practices still exist. They pose environmental, social, and economic risks. For example, many mines discard and store by-products in waste heaps or tailings pools. Those pools can be toxic and are held in place by tailings dams, which are designed to contain the mining by-products forever. Unfortunately, a fairly common (because it is inexpensive to construct) type of dam construction is also prone to failure.[118]

Here are just some of the waste heap and tailings dam failures in the 18 months immediately preceding the writing of this book:[119]

- January 2019: Brumadinho, Brazil – The dam on this iron mine collapsed, sending a tailings wave about five miles downstream and killing 259 people. Eleven are still missing. The market value of Vale, the mining company, plunged by $19 billion – or 24% – as a result of the accident.[120]
- March 2019: Machadinho d'Oeste, Brazil – This tin mine's dam collapsed after heavy rain, damaging seven bridges.
- April 2019: Muri, India – Red mud from the tailings pond at this bauxite mine spilled over 35 acres and a railway line.
- April 2019: Hpakant, Myanmar – A waste heap collapsed at this jade mine, killing three workers; 54 workers are still missing.
- July 2019: San Pedro de Coris district, Peru – The dam failure at this copper mine polluted more than ten acres.
- March 2020: Tieli, China – An overflow system at this molybdenum mine failed, endangering the supply of drinking water for some 68,000 people.
- July 2020: Hpakant, Myanmar – This jade mine waste heap failure killed at least 126 people.

Galvanized by the Brumadinho disaster, a coalition of asset owners and asset managers, with an aggregate $13 trillion under management, formed the Investor Mining and Tailings Safety Initiative.[121] Co-chaired by the Church of England Pensions Board and the Ethics Council of the Swedish AP Funds, the investor coalition midwifed new safety and disclosure standards in just two years.

Following input from technical advisors, governments, the extractive industry, and local communities, the coalition held several high-level investor and industry meetings as both fact finding and sensitizing exercises. The investors then created two major initiatives. First, they advocated for "a new independent and publicly accessible international standard for tailings dams based upon the consequences of failure."[122] The resultant review and standard-setting initiative, co-convened by the Principles for Responsible Investing, the United Nations Environment Programme, and the International Council of Mining and Metals, issued the Global Industry Standard on Tailings Management in 2020.[123]

Second, the investor coalition tackled the lack of transparency around tailings and mining by-product storage. For example, there was no database or inventory of all tailing dams globally. The investor coalition wrote to 727 extractive companies, seeking specific, public disclosures about tailings dams and safety initiatives. Those letters were sent in April 2019. A year later, 340 had responded, of which 298 had completed their disclosures (42 asked for extra time). Perhaps more importantly, 45 of the top 50 mining companies by market capitalization had responded, and 65% of the industry has now fully and publicly disclosed the information.[124]

Legitimacy

The wide variety of issues subject to third stage governance focus – many of which are politically fraught – raises the question of what is a "legitimate" issue for beta activism?[125] Defining legitimacy is not a trivial question. For example, the US Department of Labor has issued dueling guidance relating to the use of ESG metrics and specifically labelled ESG funds in pension plans, with changes in diametrically opposed directions after different political parties won election.[126] Unfortunately, most of the discussion around what is and what is not legitimate has been framed by politics and influenced by outmoded MPT ideas of what is and what is not "investing" ignores the idea that not undertaking beta activism has its own risks: If AMR really results in the loss of 10 million lives and $100 trillion in economic destruction, is choosing not to act a value neutral decision? That not acting is still making a decision only justifies beta activism generically, however. What determines the validity of any one specific beta activist campaign?

We define legitimacy as improving the fulfilment of investing's twin purposes, as defined in chapter 2 of creating a risk-adjusted return for investors and intermediation/capital allocation for society. We extend those purposes by including the concepts of extended risk/return and extended intermediation (chapter 4). Illegitimacy, then, would be that which benefits an individual's or organization's idiosyncratic beliefs or economic advantage and/or negatively affects risk/return maximization or intermediation. Certainly, there is a possibility of private capture of stage three governance activities. However, there are inherent guard-rails that would seem to provide some (although not absolute) protection against the abuse of beta activism.

Beta activists, by definition, try to affect systematic issues. That means that they need to influence multiple parties, both within and outside capital markets. (Hence the importance of "interconnectedness" as a tool of intentionality.) As any risk manager will tell you, frauds and abuses are more difficult to accomplish if the instigator needs to corrupt multiple parties. Therefore, the need to engage multiple investors, companies, regulators, the press, NGOs, academics, and others is an important barrier to beta activism being used for private gain at the expense of the environmental, social, and financial systems. After all, those parties benefit from improvements to the systems and would need, somehow, to be compensated to participate in an "illegitimate" beta activist effort that would harm them. Compounding that safeguard is the fact that beta activists usually represent a small portion of the capital market. An investment manager like Domini represents less than two hundredths of a basis point of the capital markets. (Even BlackRock, the largest fund manager in the world, represents less than 7 percent.) That means that a beta activist generally must make a broad economic argument to the other capital market participants as well as to the real economy players to get them to act. It is hard to envision that a private economic benefit ("investor opportunism" in polite corporate governance speak) argument would be persuasive.

In addition, beta activists themselves, whether asset managers or asset owners, have governance structures. Boards of directors or trustees or investment committees generally need to approve such activities. In our experience, they ask for the economic justification of the activities before approving the expenditure of resources, and such actions are rarely undertaken lightly.

Finally, regulatory regimes around the world, from the UK's stewardship code to the USA's N-PX proxy disclosure, force investors to provide some level of transparency about their proxy voting, engagement, and stewardship activities. While transparency is not an absolute bar to bad behavior, it is a deterrent.

The Economics of Beta Activism

The market's beta might be set at 1.0 to measure individual security's or portfolio's movements relative to the overall market, but, as we discussed in chapter two, what that 1.0 represents varies over time, reflecting the universe of investors' views and capital deployment. "Risk on" markets occur when investors demand less compensation for investing because they anticipate lower risk in the future. "Risk off" markets are the opposite. Surprises that are viewed to increase risk in the future – for example, the coronavirus in 2020 or the global financial crisis in 2008 – result in market-wide decreases in asset values. Similarly, expectations of decreased risk, such as the decreased possibility of armed conflict or a cut in central bank interest rates designed to increase economic activity, result in market-wide increases in asset values. Therefore, any mitigation of systematic risk resulting from stage three governance actions should result in increased asset values. It is, in effect, the counter to hyper-discounting of future cash flows or pulling risk forward irrationally.

That rerating of risk is powerful. For example, as detailed in chapter two, New York City's. Boardroom Accountability Project was viewed by investors as decreasing governance risk across 75 companies. That one initiative resulted in a 53-basis-point re-rating.

That quantitative evaluation makes the New York City BAP rare, if not unique. It was enabled by the on-again-off-again-proxy-access natural experiment. More commonly, calculating the quantitative impact of stage three governance activities is difficult, as there is no "control" group, precisely because the attempted mitigation of systematic risk is designed to affect the entire market, not just a subset of it, so there is no control group. That creates a contra-factual situation for analysis.

Of course, even in those cases without control groups, we have some data points. For instance, when looking at gender discrimination, we have a McKinsey study showing implied valuation differences worth tens of billions of dollars between top-quartile and bottom-quartile firms when it comes to gender diversity issues.[127] And we have estimates of the cost of risk left unmitigated; for example the $100 trillion cost of antimicrobial resistance by 2050, according to a review by the British government.[128] And, of course, we have the real-world impacts when risks metastasize, such as the 24 percent hit to Vale's market capitalization following the Brumadinho tailings dam collapse.

Therefore, even while we acknowledge the difficulty of measuring stage three governance activities' economic impact, we are willing to make an educated and, so we think, conservative estimate. In doing so, we believe that the BAP research provides some guidelines. The BAP related only to US equity markets (although there are systematic governance efforts underway in most markets).

In addition, given that a) the BAP was only one set of actions relating to one specific governance risk; b) the academic analysts judged that its impact would be larger were proxy access applied more broadly (as has happened since); c) stage three activism has expanded to such systematic risk mitigation targets as the six detailed; and d) more and larger investors (such as BlackRock, SSGA, LGIM, and GPIF) are now taking up stage three's tools of intentionality, our conservative estimate is that stage three risk mitigation efforts have probably caused, and will continue to cause, a market re-rating of at least 2−5 percent. Global assets under management at the beginning of 2020 are estimated at between $89 trillion[129] and $102 trillion,[130] and PwC estimates that global assets under management will grow to $145.4 trillion in 2025.[131] Therefore, if we use $100 trillion as an intermediate number, that means that stage three corporate governance activities have created at least $2 trillion–5 trillion in global wealth. To be certain, this is a rough estimate, but it does seem clear that third stage governance activities have added a non-trivial amount to global assets under management − and multiples of that for society and the economy as a whole.

Those numbers suggest why stage three governance is important for society and for the ultimate investors, whether individuals or institutional asset owners. It is also impactful to the asset management industry, as the industry's most common fee structure is based on assets under management. There are many estimates of industry average fees, with most ranging from between 50 basis points to 1 percent[132] which means stage three governance activities are worth between $10 billion–50 billion annually to the industry.

However, the benefit to the industry as a whole does not neatly translate to any individual firm. Because the impacts of stage three governance are market-wide, this does not allow firms to differentiate themselves the way trading (alpha-seeking) does. This is a traditional "free rider" problem, in which those firms that do not contribute to stage three corporate governance activities will still benefit, to the extent that they share in the extra fees generated by the overall 2–5 percent increase in assets under management. The free rider issue has been a pest to corporate governance experts since stage one. In 2003 Tom Jones, the head of Citicorp's asset management unit, noted that "if we spend money to do shareholder activism, Citigroup asset management shareholders bear the expense but don't get a benefit that is distinct from other shareholders."[133] Notably, Jones did not deny the benefits; he just valued the commercial benefits to Citigroup as a firm above those to his beneficiaries.

Thankfully, that attitude is changing. Contrast Jones's 2003 statement with what LGIM's Sacha Sadan told a finance seminar at Cambridge in 2020. "We have £750 million in BP (stock). Are you saying I shouldn't care about that £750 million just because someone else might benefit as well?"[134]

Sadan's focus was on the firm's obligations to its clients. But even a theoretically amoral asset manager, who ignores its obligations to the savers who have entrusted their money to it, should be supportive of third stage corporate governance, for purely self-interested reasons. First, as more and more stewardship codes, other reporting regimes, and institutional asset owners ask what investment firms are doing to deal with risk, firms that do not embrace third stage corporate governance will find themselves left behind, which could make it difficult to compete for institutional mandates. Already, being a PRI signatory is a de facto standard for being considered for many institutional investing mandates.

One way to think about it is that being supportive of third stage corporate governance is doing your part to ensure that there is 2–5 percent more assets to manage than there would be otherwise. Another, more self-interested framing is that third stage governance activities are an inexpensive insurance policy. Here is the math for an asset management firm:

Optimal spend on governance activities = (AUM*average fee) (100 − target net margin/100)(0.02 to 0.05)

As an example, take Manager X, whose average fee is 50 basis points and which has $10 billion in assets under management, resulting in gross fees of $50 million. This manager boasts a net margin of 40 percent across its business. Manager X should spend between $600,000 and $1.5 million ($50,000,000)(0.6)(0.02 to 0.05) on third stage corporate governance activities. Of course, there are contextual issues that would adjust the amount for each manager. For managers with little in assets under management, there is a minimum expense required that will manifest as a step function, as each new hire or initiative represents a quantum of expense necessary to be effective. At the other end of the scale, there is the practical question of how to productively put tens of millions of dollars to work for a mega manager. And there are business model questions. For instance, a responsible investing manager that features stewardship activities as core to its identity might spend more.

In addition, there are ways to mitigate the free rider issue. Various types of coalitions have formed to reduce the cost of collective actions for any one participant, as well as to aggregate assets. to have an impact. As examples, CERES[135] and Climate Action 100[136] focus on environmental issues, while the Investor Stewardship Group[137] and the International Corporate Governance Network[138] focus on governance issues and sustainability more broadly. National groups, such as the Council of Institutional Investors[139] in the USA, Instituto Brasileiro Governança Corporativa in Brazil, and the Canadian Coalition for Good Governance[140] in Canada, provide more in-depth single market coverage. PRI provides for collective engagements around the world. These coordinated engagements with leading and supporting investors seem to work, according to academic research.[141]

Oscar Wilde Was Correct

Combining third-stage governance activities and its systems focus with security selection and portfolio diversification would seem to solve the MPT paradox, at least partly. Beta activism allows investors to mitigate systematic risks somewhat and take advantage of systematic opportunities.

Sometimes, because the asset management industry is concerned with deploying, overseeing, and disposing of financial assets, analyses of the industry are limited to issues of market price. However, as stage three governance activities are designed to affect the social, financial, and environmental systems and how they create/destroy value/risk, solely measuring capital market price simply because price can be measured more easily and exactly than systems' health recalls the definition of Oscar Wilde's cynic, which could be applied to an asset manager: "A man who knows the price of everything but the value of nothing."[142]

As eye-popping as the $2 trillion to $5 trillion in value-created figure might be, the non-asset price impacts of stage three corporate governance are multiples greater, particularly when considering the extended risk mitigation and extended intermediation/asset allocation impacts. Third stage corporate governance activities do not assume, as MPT does, that creating a least variance portfolio out of the available options is somehow societally positive or sustains the financial, environmental, and social systems. Rather, third stage governance actively seeks to bolster those systems. As Scottish investor and social entrepreneur David Pitt Watson wrote, in response to an early draft of this chapter, without investors enforcing accountability on those to whom power is entrusted, "capital markets will fail."[143]

To succeed in the long term, investors need the environmental, social, and financial systems on which the capital markets rely to be robust and sustainable. As we have written elsewhere, "To assume that the long-run is a series of short-runs − and that the current systemic risk context will remain in place and acceptable − assumes that people act in responsible ways for the long-run to protect the essential systems that allow capital markets to function… We argue that systems are somewhat path dependent, with the next evolution of the system dependent on its current state rather than somehow mean regressing to a normal or standard state. Put somewhat differently, the long-term is not simply additive short-term intervals, each of which is unrelated to the previous and the next. Rather, it is the linkages of various past and current events to future ones."[144] To put this in MPT terms, these are not random events and therefore not random walks. Rather, their directions are probabilistic and causally linked.

These, then, are the advantages of adding third stage corporate governance to MPT: The ability to mitigate systematic risks to the real world's financial, social, and environmental systems, thereby causing the capital markets to re-rate and creating trillions of dollars in value − and, most importantly, the ability to keep those systems functioning in future.

Notes

1   See, for example, Paul Frentrop. "A History of Corporate Governance," Deminor, 2003.
2   Ibid. Frentrop.
3   Gelderblom, Oscar, Abe de Jong, and Joost Jonker. "An Admiralty for Asia: Isaac Le Maire and Conflicting Conceptions About the Corporate Governance of the

VOC" (July 6, 2010). ERIM Report Series Reference No. ERS-2010-026-F&A. Available at: https://ssrn.com/abstract=1633247.

4   Jonathan G.S. Koppell. "Origins of Shareholder Advocacy," Palgrave MacMillan, 2011, pp. 1–2.

5   J.G. van Dillen, Geoffrey Poitras, and Asha Majithia. "Isaac LeMaire and the early trading in Dutch East India Company Shares," in *Pioneers of Financial Economics*, Vol. I, Edward Elgar Publishing (2006), p. 58.

6   *Op cit*. Koppell, p. 2.

7   See, generally, Adolf Berle and Gardiner Means. *The Modern Corporation and Private Property*. Transaction Publishers, 1932.

8   Adam Smith. *The Wealth of Nations*. Edinburgh: Brown and Nelson (reprinted 1827), p. 311.

9   Robert A.G. Monks and Nell Minow. *Corporate Governance*. Blackwell Publishing, 4th ed., 2007, p 266.

10 Drucker, Peter F. *Management: Tasks, Responsibilities, Practices*. New York, NY: HarperCollins, 1974, p. 628.

11 Barry Barbash, Director, Division of Investment Management, SEC, speech before the ICI Securities Law Procedures Conference, December 4, 1997.

12 Luis A. Aguilar, SEC Commissioner. Speech to Georgia State University, J. Mack Robinson College of Business, April 19, 2013.

13 James P. Hawley. "Political Voice, Fiduciary Activism, and the Institutional Ownership of US Corporations: The Role of Public and Non-corporate Pension Funds," *Sociological Perspectives* Vol. 38, No. 3 (1995).

14 Charles McGrath. "80% of equity market cap held by institutions," Pensions & Investments, April 25, 2017.

15 Few people realized the changes that institutionalization of assets would have. One who did was Peter Drucker, who wrote *The Unseen Revolution: How Pension Fund Socialism Came To America* in 1976.

16 Michael Parrish. "Occidental Ends Lawsuits Over Cost of Buyout: Settlement: Oxy will pay $3.65 million to shareholders who objected to the price David Murdock got for his shares in 1984," *Los Angeles Times*, March 21, 1992.

17 J.P. Hicks. "Goodyear Buys Out Goldsmith," *The New York Times*, November 21, 1986.

18 "Quaker State Buys Back Shares from Steinberg," United Press International, March 30, 1984.

19 M.A. Ravindranath. "Saul P. Steinberg Dies at 73; Corporate Raider Amassed Multiple Fortunes," *The Washington Post*, December 11, 2012.

20 J.R. Macey, and F. McChesney. "A Theoretical Analysis of Corporate Greenmail," *Yale Law Journal*, Vol. 95, No. 1 (1985).

21 F. R. Bleakley. "Tough State Treasurer: Jesse Unruh; A Trustee Takes on the Greenmailers," *The New York Times*, February 10, 1985.

22 Co-author Lukomnik was staff to Harrison J. Goldin, the New York City Comptroller, at the time. Goldin, together with Unruh and New Jersey State Treasurer Roland Machold were the initial co-Chairs of the Council of Institutional Investors.

23 www.cii.org. Accessed June 17, 2020.

24 David A. Vise. "Bill of Rights Seeks to Boost Power of Shareholders," *The Washington Post*, April 13, 1986.

25 Ibid.

26 See John Holusha. "Company News; Pension Funds Irked at GM," *The New York Times*, December 18, 1986 and William Glaberson, "Company News; Head of GM Sees End of Perot Controversy," *The New York Times*, January 29, 1987. Goldin's quote was not included but was referred to in Glaberson's article.

27 Vineeta Anand. "The Names That Made Corporate Governance: Key Players Saw Shift From Faceoff To Cooperation," *Pensions & Investments*, February 23, 1998.

28   Jon Lukomnik. "Thoughts on the Origins and Development of the Modern Corporate Governance Movement and Shareholder Activism," Chapter 22, *The Handbook of Corporate Governance*, Richard LeBlanc, ed., John Wiley & Sons (2016).

29   *Op cit.* Anand.

30   James P. Hawley and Jon Lukomnik. "The third, systems stage of corporate governance: Why institutional investors need to move beyond modern portfolio theory." Available at https://papers.ssrn.com/sol3/papers.cfm?abstract_id=3127767. Accessed February 28, 2020.

31   S.L. Nesbitt. "The CalPERS Effect: A Corporate Governance Update," Wilshire Associates, 1995.

32   J. Van Heeckeren. "Managers' Journal; Why Investors Push for Strong Corporate Boards," *Asian Wall Street Journal*, June 30, 1997.

33   "Wilshire: 'CalPERS Effort' improves company stock performance," *Pensions & Investments*, October 10, 2013.

34   Ben Laurance and John Hooper, *et al.* "Maxwell's body found in sea", *The Guardian*, November 6, 1991. Accessed September 11, 2020.

35   Steven Prokesch. "Maxwell's Mirror Group Has $727.5 Million Loss," *The New York Times*. June 24, 1992. Accessed September 9, 2020.

36   The Bank of Commerce and Credit International was another financial fraud and scandal at that time.

37   Report of the Committee on The Financial Aspects of Corporate Governance, The Committee on the Financial Aspects of Corporate Governance and Gee and Co. Ltd, December 1992.

38   Ibid.

39   Ira Millstein, Michael Albert, Sir Adrian Cadbury, Robert E. Denham, Dieter Feddersen, and Nobuo Tatesi. "Corporate Governance: Improving Competitiveness and Access to Capital in Global Markets," OECD, 1998.

40   *OECD Corporate Governance Handbook 2019*, p. 29.

41   Ibid.

42   Hermes Pension Management, *The Hermes Principles*, London, 2002.

43   Ibid.

44   *Op cit.* Anand.

45   Ibid.

46   See https://trilliuminvest.com/about. Accessed October 18, 2020.

47   For a short history of the oil spill, see www.history.com/topics/1980s/exxon-valdez-oil-spill. Accessed February 28, 2020.

48   Stephen Davis, Jon Lukomnik, and David Pitt-Watson. *The New Capitalists*, Harvard Business School Press, 2006, p. 160.

49   Ibid.

50   Ibid.

51   See www.globalreporting.org/information/about-gri/gri-history/Pages/GRI's%20history.aspx. Accessed February 28, 2020.

52   www.unpri.org/pri/about-the-pri/322.article. Accessed June 17, 2020.

53   Sustainable Investments Institute. "Fact Sheet: Social and Environmental Shareholder Proposals at US Companies," January 2020. Available at: https://siinstitute.org/reports.html. Accessed February 28, 2020.

54   Martin Skancke. "The Government Pension Fund Global and the management of petroleum wealth," Norwegian Ministry of Finance, June 2010.

55   Douglas Appell. "GPIF hopes to use size as a way to enhance beta," *Pensions & Investments*, November 27, 2017.

56   www.lgim.com/uk/en/capabilities/corporate-governance/stewardship-and-integration. Accessed February 28, 2020.

57 Comments of Sacha Sadan, LGIM Director of Corporate Governance, to PhD Finance class, Cambridge Judge Business School, University of Cambridge, February 25, 2020.

58 See, for example, Christian May. "Why Legal and General is trying to slay the chair and CEO role," *City AM*, February 4, 2020. Available at: www.cityam.com/legal-general-has-an-appetite-for-change. Accessed March 2, 2020.

59 Stephen Davis and Jon Lukomnik. "Dreaming the Impossible Corporate Governance Dream," *Compliance Week*, July 8, 2008.

60 Ellen C. Quigley. "Universal Ownership Theory in the Anthropocene" (2019). Available at: https://papers.ssrn.com/sol3/papers.cfm?abstract_id=3457205. Accessed June 19, 2020.

61 Quigley. "Universal Ownership in the Age of Covid-19: social norms, feedback loops, and the double hermeneutic," May 2020. Available at: https://ssrn.com/abstract=3142202, pp. 18–19.

62 Ibid, p. 16.

63 James P. Hawley and Jon Lukomnik. "The Purpose of Asset Management," Pension Insurance Corporation (2018), London.

64 Ibid.

65 "Allianz is driving change toward a low-carbon economy with an ambitious climate protection package", available at: www.allianz.com/en/press/news/business/insurance/180504-allianz-announces-climate-protection-package.html. Accessed June 20, 2020.

66 Harry M. Markowitz. "Can You Do Well While Doing Good (Part II)," *Investing for Catholics*, July 20, 2012, pp. 4–8.

67 Index providers tend to use free-float adjustments. See "Russell Global Index Construction & Methodology" and "MSCI Global Investible Markets Indices Methodology."

68 There is one theoretical case wherein the systematic exclusions of negatively skewed securities reducing the ability of a portfolio manager to optimize a portfolio: If the excluded securities are so uncorrelated to the remaining universe of investors that they could, in theory help the overall portfolio, even though they, themselves, are worse performers or more volatile. The authors believe this to be a remote possibility.

69 www.ceres.org/news-center/press-releases/investor-organizations-and-financial-industry-firms-analysis-public. Accessed September 6, 2020.

70 Email to Jon Lukomnik, July 2, 2020.

71 As pointed out in Chapter 3, as at 2020, the European Union was working on disclosure regulation to minimize "green washing" of "green bonds" and other "green" products, adding a political risk factor.

72 Tjibbe Hoesktra. "Largest Dutch schemes positive on SDG bond," *IPE Magazine*, March 2020. Available at: www.ipe.com/news/largest-dutch-schemes-positive-on-sdg-bond/10044068.article#.Xl016j7pkUc.linkedin. Accessed March 3, 2020.

73 Dan Murphy. "'Social Bonds' are surging as conscious investment turns mainstream," CNBC, June 23, 2020. Available at: www-cnbc-com.cdn.ampproject.org/c/s/www.cnbc.com/amp/2020/06/23/social-bonds-are-surging-as-conscious-investing-turns-mainstream.html. Accessed July 5, 2020.

74 Baker McKenzie. "Sustainability Finance: From Niche to the New Normal," 2020, p. 11.

75 BlackRock. Available at: www.blackrock.com/corporate/investor-relations/larry-fink-ceo-letter. Accessed January 29, 2020.

76 Bank of England. Available at: www.bankofengland.co.uk/news/2019/april/open-letter-on-climate-related-financial-risks. Accessed February 28, 2020.

77 Mark Jones and John Revill. "Central banks can't save the World from Climate Change, BIS Says," Reuters, January 20, 2020. Available at: https://uk.reuters.com/a

rticle/uk-climatechange-cenbank-bis/central-banks-cant-save-the-world-from-climate-change-bis-says-idUKKBN1ZJ1CL. Accessed January 29, 2020.

78   Attracta Mooney. "Asset managers accused of climate change hypocrisy," *Financial Times*, September 26, 2016.

79   www.ceres.org/news-center/press-releases/blackrock-joins-climate-action-100-ensure-largest-corporate-emitters-act. Accessed February 28, 2020.

80   *Op. cit.* BlackRock.

81   "State of Integrated and Sustainability Reporting 2018," Sustainable Investments Institute and IRRC Institute (2018). With the approval of the EU Taxonomy on Climate (part of the EU Action Plan on Sustainable Finance), there will be an EU-wide standardization, with global implication. The taxonomy is highly detailed, technical, and transparent.

82   Attracta Mooney and Billy Nauman. "Larry Fink rules on the best global standards for climate risk reporting," *Financial Times*, January 20, 2020.

83   Charles Schmidt and Undark. "Coronavirus Researchers Tried To Warn Us," *The Atlantic*, June 13, 2020. Available at: www.theatlantic.com/health/archive/2020/06/scientists-predicted-coronavirus-pandemic/613003. Accessed July 3, 2020.

84   https://amr-review.org/. Accessed July 3, 2020.

85   "Tackling Drug-Resistant Infections Globally: Final Report and Recommendations," *The Review on Antimicrobial Resistance*, May 2016.

86   Ibid.

87   https://amr-review.org/. *Op cit.*

88   https://preventablesurprises.com/what-we-do. Accessed July 3, 2020.

89   www.nordea.com/en/about-nordea/who-we-are/our-organisation/#anchor4. Accessed June 30, 2020.

90   www.nordea.com/sv/hallbarhet/sustainable-finance/nyheter/2016/our-engagement-counts-in-india.html?&p=11. Accessed July 3, 2020.

91   www.nordea.com/sv/hallbarhet/sustainable-finance/nyheter/2016/our-engagement-counts-in-india.html?&p=11. Accessed June 30, 2020.

92   www.europeanpharmaceuticalreview.com/article/115074/limiting-antibiotic-manufacturing-discharge-in-indian-wastewater. Accessed June 30, 2020.

93   Danielle Wiener-Bronner. "Why a defiant girl is staring down the Wall Street bull." CNNMoney, March 7, 2017. Available at: https://money.cnn.com/2017/03/07/news/girl-statue-wall-street-bull. Accessed February 28, 2020.

94   Email from State Street Global Advisors to author.

95   www.30percentcoalition.org/who-we-are. Accessed July 11, 2020.

96   Clare Payn. "Legal & General commitment to gender diversity," August 28, 2018. Available at: www.legalandgeneral.com/investments/investment-content/legal-and-general-commitment-to-gender-diversity. Accessed February 28, 2020.

97   Maggie Fitzgerald. "There is now a woman at every S&P 500 company," CNBC, July 25, 2019. Available at: www.cnbc.com/2019/07/25/there-is-now-a-woman-board-member-at-every-sp-500-company.html. Accessed March 4, 2020.

98   Anne Stych. "Women's representation on boards reaches a milestone," *Bizwomen*, September 12, 2019. Available at: www.bizjournals.com/bizwomen/news/latest-news/2019/09/womens-representation-on-boards-reaches-a.html?page=all. Accessed March 4, 2020.

99   Alisha Haridasani Gupta. "Why 2019 was a Breakthrough Year for Women in the Boardroom," *The New York Times*, March 3, 2020. Available at: www.nytimes.com/2020/03/03/us/women-company-boards-private.html. Accessed March 4, 2020.

100 Sophie Baker. "Managers continue working for balance," *Pensions & Investments*, May 18, 2020. Available at: www.pionline.com/special-report-gender-diversity/managers-continue-working-balance. Accessed June 22, 2020.

101 Vivian Hunt, Sara Prince, Sundiatu Dixon-Fyle, and Lareina Yee. "Delivering Through Diversity", McKinsey & Company, January 2018.

102   *2019 Impact Report*, Domini Funds.
103   www.domini.com/investing-for-impact/forests. Accessed July 4, 2020.
104   Ibid.
105   *Domini Impact Report*, Q1, 2020.
106   SEC form adv. https://adviserinfo.sec.gov/firm/summary/109505. Accessed July 4, 2020.
107   www.domini.com/insights/investors-support-california-act-to-protect-forests-introdu
      ced-today. Accessed July 4, 2020.
108   Kashmir Hill. "Wrongfully Accused by an Algorithm," *The New York Times*,
      June 24, 2020. Available at: www.nytimes.com/2020/06/24/technology/facial-recog
      nition-arrest.html. Accessed June 30, 2020.
109   Steve Lohr. "Facial Recognition Is Accurate, if You're a White Guy," *The New
      York Times*, February 9, 2018. Available at: www.nytimes.com/2018/02/09/technol
      ogy/facial-recognition-race-artificial-intelligence.html. Accessed July 30, 2020.
110   Hill. *Op cit.*
111   www.cnbc.com/2019/11/11/goldman-sachs-to-reevaluate-apple-card-credit-limits-a
      fter-bias-claim.html. Accessed June 30, 2020.
112   Artificial Intelligence Applications in Financial Services, 2019. www.oliverwyman.
      com/our-expertise/insights/2019/dec/artificial-intelligence-applications-in-financia
      l-services.html. Accessed June 30, 2020.
113   Financial Conduct Authority. Final Notice, Liberty Mutual Insurance Europe SE,
      October 29, 2018. www.fca.org.uk/publication/final-notices/liberty-mutual-insura
      nce-europe-se-2018.pdf. Accessed June 30, 2020.
114   www.federatedinvestors.com/about/corporate-overview.do. Accessed July 4, 2020.
115   See, for example, Chow *et al*. "Investors' Expectations on Responsible Artificial
      Intelligence and Data Governance," Hermes Investment Management, April 2019.
116   "Artificial Intelligence Applications in Financial Services," *Op cit.*
117   Public Engagement Report (Q1 2020) pp. 6–9 and Public Engagement Report (Q2
      2019), pp. 17–21.
118   www.pbs.org/wgbh/frontline/article/tailings-dams-where-mining-waste-is-stored-fo
      rever. Accessed July 11, 2020.
119   All the following tailing mine failures. Available at: www.wise-uranium.org/mdaf.
      html. Accessed July 11, 2020.
120   Paula Laier. "Vale stock plunges after Brazil disaster; $19 billion in market value lost."
      Reuters, January 28, 2019. Available at: www.reuters.com/article/us-vale-sa-disaster-
      stocks/vale-stock-plunges-after-brazil-disaster-19-billion-in-market-value-lost-idUSK
      CN1PM1JP. Accessed July 12, 2020.
121   www.churchofengland.org/investor-mining-tailings-safety-initiative. Accessed July
      10, 2020.
122   www.churchofengland.org/investor-mining-tailings-safety-initiative. *Op cit.*
123   Aiden Davy, Chief Operating Office, International Council of Mining and Metals,
      statement on Reuters webinar, "ESG Standards: The Best Way Forward," July 9, 2020.
124   www.churchofengland.org/investor-mining-tailings-safety-initiative. *Op cit.*
125   The authors are indebted to the late Peter Montagnon for sensitizing us to this issue.
126   See, for example, David Silk and Sebastian Niles. "Department of Labor Cautionary
      Tone on ESG-Related Activities," Harvard Law School Forum on Corporate Gov-
      ernance, May 2, 2018. Available at: https://corpgov.law.harvard.edu/2018/05/02/depa
      rtment-of-labor-cautionary-tone-on-esg-related-activities/. Accessed June 20, 2020.
127   Vivian Hunt, Sara Prince, Sundiatu Dixon-Fyle, and Lareina Yee. "Delivering
      Through Diversity," McKinsey and Company, January 2018.
128   https://amr-review.org/. Accessed July 3, 2020.
129   Boston Consulting Group. "Global Assets Under Management 2020: Protect,
      Adapt, and Innovate," May 2020.
130   McKinsey & Co. "Global Trends In Asset Management," January 2020.

131   PwC. "Asset & Wealth Management Revolution: Embracing Exponential Change," 2017.

132   See, for example, "Asset Management Market Study, Interim Report: Annex 7- Fund Charges Analysis," Financial Conduct Authority (2016); "2019 Investment Company Factbook: A Review of Tends and Activities in the Investment Company Industry," Investment Company Institute (2019).

133   Davis *et al.* (2006). *Op cit.*, p. 71.

134   Sacha Sadan. Presentation to PhD Finance class, Cambridge Judge Business School, University of Cambridge, February 25, 2020.

135   www.ceres.org.

136   www.climateaction100.org.

137   www.isgframework.org.

138   www.icgn.org.

139   www.cii.org.

140   www.ccgg.ca.

141   Elroy Dimson, Oguzhan Karakas, and Xi Li. "Coordinated Engagements," 24 December 2018. Available at https://papers.ssrn.com/sol3/papers.cfm?abstract_id= 3209072. Accessed March 3, 2020.

142   Oscar Wilde. *Lady Windemere's Fan*, (1892; 1906 ed.) Boston, MA and London: John W. Luce & Company, Act 3, p. 57.

143   Email to the authors, August 29, 2020.

144   James P. Hawley and Jon Lukomnik. "The Long and Short of It: Are We Asking the Right Questions. Modern Portfolio Theory and Time Frames," *Seattle University Law Review*, Vol. 41, Issue 2 (2018).

Conclusion

Modern Portfolio Theory (MPT) and the market-dominant theories that grew up with it (efficient market hypothesis, capital asset pricing model, random walk, etc.) are both brilliant and deeply flawed. They are flawed by omissions, flawed by commissions, and flawed by self-imposed constraints. They contain a number of unreal and/or mistaken assumptions. They fail to evolve as their own performative characteristics change the capital markets.

MPT is a creature of its historical moment. That moment has long passed. While there was in the 1950s into the 1980s a plausible argument that these flaws, although problematic, allowed MPT to usher in a conceptual and practical revolution. This ironic achievement is not to be underestimated. It is ironic because various components of the MPT tradition are far too narrow to be able to address the multiple challenges that have arisen from the investment revolution that MPT itself wrought.

MPT and the associated theories were never intended to deal with systematic and systemic risk. MPT saw these risks as exogenous. But errors of omission are still errors and particularly problematic when the performative nature of those theories redefines investing into a narrow box, sealed away from the real economy and society. MPT's paradigm does not accommodate feedback loops, either conceptually or practically. MPT ignores the Values to value dynamic; it ignores (and in some cases denies) its own unwitting contributions to financial panics and crises. It has no mechanism to understand whether its impacts benefit or denigrate environmental, social, and financial systems. MPT has neither recognized the ironies of its own performative successes, nor the structural market changes partly created as a result of them.

MPT's massive successes, clearly based on Markowitz's complex math and others subsequently developing a variety of complementary techniques and strategies, have blinded most MPT practitioners to the limitations of the MPT tradition.

We titled this book "Moving beyond modern portfolio theory". We did not title it "an alternative theory to MPT," but clearly, we have alternatives in mind, most specifically discussed in chapter 5. We have long seen corporate governance activism, especially stage three activism focused on mitigating systematic and systemic risk, as a layering on to MPT's use of diversification. We do not disagree with that *per se* but note that the most important stage three governance activity might be simply broadening the definition of investing to consider systems in a way that MPT cannot. By viewing investing and the real world as in a constant feedback dialogue, third stage governance is able to spot red flag warnings ignored by MPT. That puts a spotlight on investments that potentially have significant externality effects and on system health. This suggests that when firms or whole sectors create systemic risk by "normal" operations, those investments need to be singled out. Once flagged, stage three corporate governance redefines investing to include not just security analysis, trading, and portfolio construction, but also a panoply of tools of intentionality. Stage three corporate governance investors are cognizant of the behavioral changes that they seek through their own feedback loops. That is a much more self-aware and nuanced dynamic than MPT's willful blindness to all but price, volatility, and correlation.

When we began a series of talks, blogs, papers, and articles about MPT's limitations in 2015, we did not realize how much the world was changing under our feet and how rapidly it would change by the time we finished writing this book in late 2020. In the midst of such rapid change, it is difficult to properly assess all that is actually going on around you. More and more investment professionals of all types have come to embrace a focus on systemic risk. Many more have begun to think that the MPT tradition does not and cannot explain what is going on; they have come to agree with the limitations of the MPT tradition and are actively looking to evolve in practice and theory. Even more have adopted some form of ESG integration or impact investing; a common "on-ramp" for those who ultimately come to think about the interaction of environmental, social, and financial systems and capital markets.

"Moving beyond MPT" means recognizing the complex relations between investing and systems and attempting to mitigate systematic and systemic risks alike. Investing that matters, which we believe is becoming the "new normal," must therefore come to embrace MPT's focus on diversification and risk-adjusted return, but understand them as relevant to the needs of investors and the economy as a whole, rather than relative to the extant capital markets. We need to move beyond the hermetically sealed math that says a portfolio manager has done well if the portfolio outperforms a benchmark, even if the total return is negative, or if the investment itself contributes to a negative externality which deteriorates the conditions of life in which the return from the portfolio will be expended. Extended risk and extended intermediation need to be factored into day-to-day investment and trading decisions, as well as into stage three governance activities. This is what "investing that matters" means.

Bibliography

Aguilar, Luis A. (2013) Commissioner, Securities and Exchange Commission, Speech to Georgia State University, April 19, 2013. Available at: www.sec.gov/news/speech/2013-spch041913laahtm.

Ambachtsheer, K. (2006) "Alpha, Beta, Barrlegab: Investment theory of marketing strategy," *Ambaschtsheer Letter*.

Anand, V. (1998) "The Names That Made Corporate Governance: Key Players Saw Shift From Faceoff To Cooperation," *Pensions & Investments*.

Appel, Ian; Gormley, Todd; & Keim, Donald. (2014) "Passive Investors, Not Passive Owners.' Available at: https://papers.ssrn.com/sol3/Papers.cfm?abstract_id=2475150.

Austin, Duncan. (2020) "Pigou and the Dropped Stitch of Economics," February 2020. Available at: https://preventablesurprises.com/wp-content/uploads/2020/02/Pigou-and-The-Dropped-Stitch-of-Economics.pdf.

Azevedo, Mary Ann. (2019) "*Untapped Opportunity: Minority Founders Still Being Overlooked*". CrunchBase News (February 27). Available at: https://news.crunchbase.com/news/untapped-opportunity-minority-founders-still-being-overlooked.

Baker, S. (2020) "Managers continue working for balance,", *Pensions & Investments*.

Baker McKenzie. (2020) "Sustainability Finance: From Niche to the New Normal," Report. Chicago, IL: Baker McKenzie.

Barbash, B.(1997) Speech before the ICI Securities Law Procedures Conference.

Bender, Jennifer; Briand, Remy Melas, Melas, Dimitris; & Subramanian, Raman Aylur. (2015) "Foundations of Factor Investing." Available at: https://papers.ssrn.com/sol3/papers.cfm?abstract_id=2543990.

Berle, Adolph & Means, Gardiner. (1932) *The Modern Corporation and Private Property*. New York, NY: Macmillan.

Bernstein, Peter F. (2007) *Capital Ideas Evolving*. New York, NY: John Wiley & Sons.

Beslik, S. (2021) "Our engagement counts in India,", Nordea Blog. Available at: www.nordea.com/sv/hallbarhet/sustainable-finance/nyheter/2016/our-engagement-counts-in-india.html?&p=11.

Bhandari, T.; Iliev, P.; & Kalodimos, J. (2019) "Governance Changes through Shareholder Initiatives: The Case of Proxy Access' Fourth Annual Conference on Financial Market Regulation." Available at: https://ssrn.com/abstract=2635695.

Bhidé, A. (2010) *A Call for Judgment: Sensible Finance for a Dynamic Economy*. Oxford: Oxford University Press.

Bleakley, F.R. (1985) *Tough State Treasurer: Jesse Unruh; A Trustee Takes on the Greenmailers' New York Times*.

Bookstaber, Rick. (2007) "The Myth of Noncorrelation," September 23, 2007. Available at: http://rick.bookstaber.com/2007/09/myth-of-noncorrelation.html.

Breslau, Daniel. (2003) "Economics invests the economy: Mathematics, statistics and models in the work of Irving Fisher and Wesley Mitchell," *Theory and Society*, 32(3).

Briand, R. (2015) "Can ESG Add Alpha", MSCI Blog, www.msci.com/www/blog-posts/can-esg-add-alpha-/0182820893.

Brinson, G.P Hood, R.; & Beerbower, G. (1986) "Determinants of Portfolio Performance," *Financial Analysts Journal*, 42(4): 39–44.

Buffett, Warren. (2002) "Chairman's Letter". Available at: www.berkshirehathaway.com/letters/2002pdf.pdf.

Busco Cristiano; Consolandi, Costanza; Eccles, Robert G.; & Sofra, Elena (2020) "A preliminary Analysis of SASB Reporting: Disclosure Topics, Financial Relevance, and the Financial Intensity of ESG Materiality". *Journal of Applied Corporate Finance*." 32(2). Available at: https://papers.ssrn.com/sol3/papers.cfm?abstract_id=3548849.

Caldecott, Ben. (2019) "'Encourages laziness and disincentives ambition': Ben Caldecott shares his thoughts on the EU's green taxonomy." *Responsible Investor* (June). Available at: www.responsible-investor.com/articles/encourages-laziness-and-disincentives-ambition-ben-caldecott-shares-his-tho.

Campbell H. R. and Liu, Y. (2019) "A Census of the Factor Zoo," Working Paper. Available at: https://ssrn.com/abstract=3341728.

Carney, M. & Villeroy de Galhau, F. (2019) "Open letter on climate-related financial risks." London: Bank of England.

Carter, R.M.; Meyer, J.M. & Huettel, S.A. (2010) "Functional Neuroimaging of Intertemporal Choice Models: A Review," *Journal of Neuroscience, Psychology and Economics*, 3(1): 27–45.

Chamberlain, Gary & Rothschild, Michael. (1983) "Arbitrage, Factor Structure, and Mean-Variance Analysis on Large Asset Markets," *Econometrica*, 5 (5): 1281–1314.

Cheema-Fox, Alex; LaPerla, Bridget R; Serafeim, George; & Wang, Hui (Stacie). (2020) "Corporate resilience and Response during COVID-19," June. Available at: https://papers.ssrn.com/sol3/papers.cfm?abstract_id=3578167.

Chen, Nai-Fu; Roll, Richard; & Ross, Stephen A. (1986) "Economic Forces and the Stock Market," *Journal of Business*, 59(3): 383–403.

Cho, T. (2019) "Turning Alphas Into Betas: Arbitrage and Endogenous Risk," *Journal of Financial Economics*. (Forthcoming).

Chow, C.; Frame, K.; Likhtman, S.; Spooner, N.; & Wong, J. (2019) "Investors' Expectations on Responsible Artificial Intelligence and Data Governance," Report. London: Hermes Investment Management.

Church of England. (2020) "Information on the Investor Mining and Tailings Safety Initiative." Available at: www.churchofengland.org/investor-mining-tailings-safety-initiative.

Claessens, Stijn & Yafeh, Yishay (2011) "Additional to market indices and the comovement of stock returns around the world," IMF Working Paper, March.

Cochrane, John H. (2011) "*Discount Rates*," NBER working paper 16972. Available at: www.nber.org/papers/w16972.

Cohen, Patricia. (2018) "We all have a stake in the stock market, right? Guess again," *The New York Times* (February 18). Available at: www.nytimes.com/2018/02/08/business/economy/stocks-economy.html.

Committee on The Financial Aspects of Corporate Governance. (1992) "Report of the Committee on the Financial Aspects of Corporate Governance." London: The Committee on the Financial Aspects of Corporate Governance and Gee and Co. Ltd.

Consolandi Costanza; Eccles, Robert G; & Gabbi, Giampaolo. (2020) "Better Few but Belter: stock returns and the financial relevance and financial of materiality." (April). Available at: https://papers.ssrn.com/sol3/papers.cfm?abstract_id=3574547.

Coase, R.H. (1960) "The Problem of Social Costs," *The Journal of Law and Economics* (Vol. III): 1–44.

Cremers, M.; Pareet, A.; & Sautner, A. (2013) "Stock Duration and Misvaluation," Working Paper, University of Amsterdam.

Cremers, M. & Pareek, A. (2015) "Patient Capital Outperformance: The Investment Skill of High Active Share Managers Who Trade Infrequently," *Journal of Financial Economics*, (Forthcoming).

Cremers, Martijin; Pareek, Ankur; & Sautner, Zacharias. (2017) "Short-term institutions, analysts recommendation and mispricing." Available at: https://papers.ssrn.com/sol3/papers.cfm?abstract_id=2190437&rec=1&srcabs=2285470&alg=1&pos=8.

Davis, S. & Lukomnik, J. (2008) "Dreaming the Impossible Corporate Governance Dream," *Compliance Week*.

Davis, S.; Lukomnik, J.; & Pitt-Watson, D. (2006) *The New Capitalists*. Boston, MA: Harvard Business School Press.

Davis, S.; Lukomnik, J.; & Pitt-Watson, D. (2016) *What They Do With Your Money: How the Financial System Fails Us and How to Fix It*. New Haven, NJ: Yale University Press.

De La Cruz, A.; Medina, A.; and Tang Y. (2019) *Owners of the World's Listed Companies*." Paris: OECD Capital Market Series.

Dichev, I.D. (2004) "What are Stock Investors' Actual Historical Returns? Evidence from Dollar-Weighted Returns," Working Paper.

Dimson, E.; Karakas, O.; & Li, X. (2018) 'Coordinated Engagements,' Working Paper. Available at: https://papers.ssrn.com/sol3/papers.cfm?abstract_id=3209072.

Domini Funds. (2019) Impact Report. New York, NY.

Domini Funds, (2020a) "The Domini Forest Project' Blog." Available at www.domini.com/investing-for-impact/forests.

Domini Funds. (2020b) 'Investors Support California Act to Protect Forests Introduced Today,' *Blog*. Available at: www.domini.com/insights/investors-support-california-act-to-protect-forests-introduced-today.

Doyle, T. (2018) "Politics Over Performance, The Politicization of the New York City Retirement System," Washington, DC: American Council for Capital Formation.

Drucker, P.F. (1974) *Management: Tasks, Responsibilities, Practices*. New York: HarperCollins.

Drucker, P.F. (1976) *The Unseen Revolution: How Pension Fund Socialism Came to America*. New York, NY: Harper & Rowe.

Dupré, Stan. (2020) "The EU's Risky Green Taxonomy," *Project Syndicate* (January). Available at: www.project-syndicate.org/commentary/european-union-green-taxonomy-three-questions-by-stan-dupre-2020-01?barrier=accesspaylog.

Earl, Peter. (2001) *The Legacy of Herbert Simon in Economic Analysis*. Northampton, MA: Edward Elgar Publishing.

Eccles, Robert G. & Tim Youmans. (2015) "Materiality in Corporate Governance: The Statement of Significant Audiences and Materiality." Harvard Business School Working Paper, No. 16–023, September.

Edelman. *(2019)* "Edelman Trust Barometer" Available at: www.edelman.com/sites/g/files/aatuss191/files/201904/2019_Edelman_Trust_Barometer_Financial_Services_Report_1.pdf.

European Commission (2019). "Consultation document on the Update of the Non-Binding Guidelines on Non-Financial Reporting." Available at: https://ec.europa.eu/info/sites/info/files/business_economy_euro/banking_and_finance/documents/2019-non-financial-reporting-guidelines-consultation-document_en.pdf.

European Commission. (n.d.) "Sustainable Finance." Available at: https://ec.europa.eu/info/business-economy-euro/banking-and-finance/sustainable-finance_en.

Ferguson, N. (2008) *The Ascent of Money*. London: Penguin Press.

Financial Conduct Authority. (2016) "Asset Management Market Study, Interim report: Annex 7: Fund Charges Analysis." London: Financial Conduct Authority.

Financial Conduct Authority. (2018) "Liberty Mutual Insurance Europe SE," Final Notice. Available at: www.fca.org.uk/publication/final-notices/liberty-mutual-insurance-europe-se-2018.pdf.

Fink, L. (2020) "Dear CEO Letter," Blackrock Webpost. Available at: www.blackrock.com/corporate/investor-relations/larry-fink-ceo-letter.

Fitzgerald, M. (2019) "There is now a woman at every S&P 500 company," CNBC.

Fox, A.C.; LaPerlaB.R.; Serafeim, G.; & Wang, H. (2020) "Corporate Resilience and Response during COVID-19," Harvard Working Paper Series, No. 20–108.

Fox, Justin. (2009) *The Myth of the Rational Market*. New York, NY: Harper Business.

Frentrop, P., (2003) *A History of Corporate Governance*. Amsterdam: Deminor.

Friede, G.; Busch, T.; & Bassen, A. (2015) "ESG and Financial Performance: Aggregated Evidence from More than 2000 Empirical Studies," *Journal of Sustainable Finance & Investment*, 5(4): 210–233.

Friedman, Milton. (1966) "The methodology of positive economics," in *Essays in Positive Economics*. Chicago, IL: University of Chicago. Available at: http://kimoon.co.kr/gmi/reading/friedman-1966.pdf.

Friedman, Milton. (1970) "The social responsibility of the business is to increase profits." Available at: http://umich.edu/~thecore/doc/Friedman.pdf.

Gavett, G. (2012), "Tailings Dams: Where Mining Waste Is Stored Forever," PBS Frontline.

Gilson, Ronald J. & Kraakman, Reinier. (1984) "The mechanism of market efficiency," *Virginia Law Review*, 70(4): 549–644.

Glaberson, W. (1987) "Company News; Head of GM Sees End of Perot Controversy," *The New York Times*.

Gupta, A.H. (2020) "Why 2019 was a Breakthrough Year for Women in the Boardroom," *The New York Times*.

Guyat, D. & Lukomnik, J. (2010) "Does Portfolio Turnover Exceed Expectations?", *Rotman International Journal of Pension Management*, 3(2): 40–45.

Haldane, A.G. & Davies, R. (2011) "The Short Long," Speech before the 29th Société Universitaire Européenne de Recherches Financières Colloquium, "New Paradigm in Money and Finance?".

Harvey, Campbell R. & Liu, Yan. (2019) "A Census of the Factor Zoo". Available at: https://ssrn.com/abstract=3341728 and http://dx.doi.org/10.2139/ssrn.3341728.

Hawley, J.P. (1995) "Political Voice, Fiduciary Activism, and the Institutional Ownership of US Corporations: The Role of Public and Non-corporate Pension Funds," *Sociological Perspectives*, 38(3): 415–435.

Hawley, J.P. & Lukomnik, J. (2018) "The third, systems stage of corporate governance: Why institutional investors need to move beyond modern portfolio theory", Working Paper, https://papers.ssrn.com/sol3/papers.cfm?abstract_id=3127767.

Hawley J.P. & Lukomnik, J. (2018) *The Purpose of Asset Management*. London: Pension Insurance Corporation.

Hawley, J P. & Lukomnik, J. (2018) "The Long and Short of It: Are We Asking the Right Questions?", *Seattle University Law Review*, 41(2): 449–474.

Hawley, J.P. & Williams, A.T. (2000) *The Rise of Fiduciary Capitalism*. Philadelphia, PA: University of Pennsylvania Press.

Henisz, W.J.; Koller T.; & Nuttall, R. (2019) "Five ways that ESG creates value' McKinsey Quarterly." www.mckinsey.com/business-functions/strategy-and-corporate-finance/our-insights/five-ways-that-esg-creates-value?cid=soc-web&fbclid=IwAR3onKpp8NgbyctliH jvZHNs7HcqFUhaKamqMamTYZYE8eE4aC10BbRgm_U.

Heinisz, W.J. & McGlinch, J. (2019) "ESG, Material Credit Events, and Credit Risk," *Journal of Applied Corporate Finance*, 31(2): 105–117.

Herbst-Bayliss, Svea & Delevingne, Lawrence. (2017) "Hedge fund traders from a legendary desk at Goldman Sachs have lost billions of dollars," Reuters, March 27.

Hereida, L.; Bartletta, S.; Carrubba, J.; Frankle, D.; Kurihara, K.; Mace, B.; Palmisani, E.; Pardasani, N.; Schulte, T.; Sheridan, B.; & Xu, Q. (2020) "Global Asset Management 2020: Protect, Adapt and Innovate,' Report, Boston Consulting Group.

Hermes Pension Management. (2002) *The Hermes Principles*. London: Hermes Pension Management.

Hicks, J.P. (1986) "Goodyear Buys Out Goldsmith," *The New York Times*.

Hill, K. (2020) "Wrongfully Accused by an Algorithm," *The New York Times*.

Hoesktra, T. (2020) "Largest Dutch schemes positive on SDG bond," *IPE Magazine*.

Holusha, J. (1986) "Company News; Pension Funds Irked at GM," *The New York Times*.

Hunt, V.; Prince, S.; Dixon-Fyle, S.; & Yee, L. (2018) "Delivering Through Diversity," McKinsey & Company.

Ibbotson, R.G. (2010) "The Importance of Asset Allocation," *Financial Analysts Journal*, 86(2): 18–20.

Investment Company Institute. (2020) *Fact Book* (60th ed.). Available at: www.icifactbook.org.

IRRC Institute and Sustainable Investments Institute. (2018) *State of Sustainability and Integrated Reporting 2018*, New York, NY.

Jegadeesh, Narasimhan & Titman, Sheridan. (1993) "Returns to Buying Winners and Selling Losers: Implications for Stock Market Efficiency," *The Journal of Finance*, 48(1).

Jones, M. & Reville, J. (2020) "Central banks can't save the world from climate change, BIS says," Reuters.

Jones, O.D. (2018) "Keynote address: Brain Science Perspectives on Investor Behavior and Decision-Making Errors," *Seattle University Law Review*, (41): 349–366.

Kahnerman, Daniel & Tversky, Amos. (1979) "Prospect theory: An analysis of decision under risk," *Econometrica*, 47(2): 263–292.

Khan, M.N.; Serafeim, G. & Yoon, A. (2015) "Corporate Sustainability: First Evidence on Materiality," Harvard Business School Working Paper, 15–073.

Koppell, J.G.S. (2011) *Origins of Shareholder Advocacy*. New York, NY: Palgrave MacMillan.

Knight, Frank. (1921) *Risk, Uncertainty and Profit*. Boston, MA: Pantianos Classics.

Kuh, Tom. (2020) "ESG After CCOVID-19: Will it be different this time?" (April). Available at: www.truvaluelabs.com/blog/esg-after-covid-19-will-it-be-different-this-time.

Laurance B. & Hooper, J (1991) "Maxwell's Body Found in Sea," *The Guardian*.

Leswing, K. (2019) "Goldman Sachs will reevaluate Apple card credit limits after bias allegations," CNBC.

Litan, Robert E. (2017) "In Defense of Most, But Not All, Financial Innovation," The Brookings Institute. Available at: www.brookings.edu/wp-content/uploads/2016/06/0217_financial_innovation_litan.pdf.

Lo, Andrew W. (2017) *Adaptive Markets: Financial evolution at the speed of thought.* Princeton, NJ: Princeton University Press.

Lohr, S. (2018) "Facial Recognition Is Accurate, If You're a White Guy,"*The New York Times*.

Lukomnik, J. (1997) "Why We Bother: A Primer in How Activism Enhances Returns," *Fordham Journal of Corporate and Financial Law*, 2(1): 1–18.

Lukomnik, J. (2016) "Thoughts on the Origins and Development of the Modern Corporate Governance Movement and Shareholder Activism," in: *The Handbook of Corporate Governance.* Hoboken, NJ: John Wiley & Sons.

Lo, Andrew W. (2017) *Adaptive Markets: Financial Evolution at the Speed of Thought.* Princeton, NJ: Princeton University Press.

J.R. Macey & McChesney F. (1985) "A Theoretical Analysis of Corporate Greenmail," *Yale Law Journal*, 95(1): 13–65.

MacKenzie, Donald. (2006) *An Engine not a Camera: How Financial Markets Shape Markets.* Cambridge, MA: MIT Press.

May, C. (2020) "Why Legal and General is trying to slay the chair and CEO role,"*City AM.*

Malinak S. & Birman S. (2020) "Performance Tests of Truvalue Labs ESG as a 6th Factor," TruValue Labs Blog.

Malkiel, Burton. *A Random Walk Down Wall Street.* (12th ed.). London: W. W. Norton & Co.

Mahmoud, O. & Meyer, J. (2020) "Sustainability in the Time of Uncertainty," Working Paper. Available at: https://papers.ssrn.com/sol3/papers.cfm?abstract_id=3597700.

Markowitz, Harry M. (1952) "Portfolio Selection," *Journal of Finance*, 7(1).

Markowitz, Harry M. (1991) "Foundations of Portfolio Theory," Nobel Lecture, December 7, 1990, in: *The Founders of Modern Finance: Their Prize-winning Concepts and 1990 Nobel Lectures.* The Research Foundation of the Institute of Chartered Finance Analysts.

Markowitz, H.M. (2012) "Can You Do Well While Doing Good (Part II)," Investing for Catholics, Irvine; Index Funds Advisors; and Investing for Catholics.

Marx, Karl. (1843–44) *Contribution to the Critique of Hegel's Philosophy of Right.* Available at: www.marxists.org/archive/marx/works/1844/df-jahrbucher/law-abs.htm.

Maslow, Abraham H. (1966) *The Psychology of Science: A Reconnaissance.* New York, NY: HarperCollins.

McGrath, Charles. (2017) "80% of equity market cap held by institutions," *Pensions & Investments*, April 25. Available at: www.pionline.com/article/20170425/INTERACTIVE/170429926/80-of-equity-market-cap-held-by-institutions.

Milhench, C. (2020a) "Public Engagement Report, Q1." London: Federated Hermes EOS.

Milhench, C. (2020b) "Public Engagement Report, Q2." London: Federated Hermes EOS.

Millstein I.; Albert M.; Cadbury A.; Denham R.L., Feddersen, D.; & Tatesi N. (1998) *Corporate Governance: Improving Competitiveness and Access to Capital in Global Markets.* Paris: OECD.

Minsky, Hyman. (1986) *Stabilizing the Unstable Economy.* New York, NY: McGraw-Hill.

Mooney, A. (2016) "Asset managers accused of climate change hypocrisy," *Financial Times*.

Mooney A. & Nauman, B. (2020) "Larry Fink rules on the best global standards for climate risk reporting," *Financial Times*.

Murphy, D. (2020) "Social Bonds' are surging as conscious investment turns mainstream," CNBC.

Nesbitt, S.L. (1985) "The CalPERS Governance Effect: A Corporate Governance Update," Wilshire Associates Report.

New York State Common Retirement Fund. (2017). "General Investment Policies." Available at: www.osc.state.ny.us/pension/generalpolicies.pdf.

OECD. (2019) *Corporate Governance Handbook*. Paris: OECD.

O'Neill, J. (2016) "Tackling Drug-Resistant Infections Globally: Final Report and Recommendations." Review on Anti-microbial Resistance, Wellcome Trust, HM Government, London.

Parrish, Michael. (1992) "Occidental Ends Lawsuits Over Cost of Buyout: Settlement: Oxy will pay $3.65 million to shareholders who objected to the price David Murdock got for his shares in 1984," *Los Angeles Times*.

Payn, C. (2019) "Legal and General Investments promotes the benefits of diversity with companies we work with," Legal and General Investments Blog. Available at: www.legalandgeneral.com/investments/investment-content/legal-and-general-commitment-to-gender-diversity.

Penaloza, Lisa & Vankatesh, Alladi. (2006) "Further evolving the new dominant logic of marketing: from services to the social construction of markets," *Marketing Theory*, 6(3).

Perold, André F. (2004). "The Capital Asset Pricing Model," *Journal of Economics, Perspectives*, 18(3).

Pitt-Watson, David & Mann, Hari. (2017) *The Purpose of Finance*. London: The Pension Insurance Corporation.

Polanyi, Karl. (1944) *The Great Transformation*. Boston, MA: Beacon Press.

Prokesch, S. (1992) "Maxwell's Mirror Group Has $727.5 Million Loss," *The New York Times*.

Quigley, E. (2019) "Universal Ownership Theory in the Anthropocene' Working Paper." Available at: https://papers.ssrn.com/sol3/papers.cfm?abstract_id=3457205.

Quigley, E. (2020) "Universal Ownership in the Age of Covid-19: social norms, feedback loops, and the double hermeneutic." Available at: https://ssrn.com/a bstract=3142202, pp. 18–19.

Rabener, N. (2019). "Warren Buffet: The Greatest Factor Investor of All Time ?", Enterprising Investor – CFA Blog. Available at: https://blogs.cfainstitute.org/investor/2019/04/15/warren-buffett-the-greatest-factor-investor-of-all-time.

Raman, J. & Lam, R. (2019) "Artificial Intelligence Applications in Financial Services," Oliver Wyman Blog. Available at: www.oliverwyman.com/our-expertise/insights/2019/dec/artificial-intelligence-applications-in-financial-services.html.

Ravindranath, M.A. (2012) "Saul P. Steinberg Dies at 73; Corporate Raider Amassed Multiple Fortunes," *The Washington Post*.

Rees, V. (2020), "Limiting antibiotic manufacturing discharge in Indian wastewater," *European Pharmaceutical Review*.

Rogers, Jean & Serafeim, George. (2019) "Pathway to Materiality: How sustainability issues become financial material to corporations and their investors," Harvard Business School Working Paper 20–056.

Ross, Stephen. (1976) "The Arbitrage Theory of Capital Asset Pricing," *Journal of Economic Theory*, 13(3): 341–360.

Routley, Nick. (2017) "Visualizing the Trillion-Fold Increase in Computing Power", *The Visual Capitalist* (November 4). Available at: www.visualcapitalist.com/visualizing-trillion-fold-increase-computing-power.

Sabri, R. (2019) "Fearless Girl: Voting Your Voice for Gender Equality Makes a Difference," Triple Pundit Blog. Available at: www.triplepundit.com/story/2019/fearless-girl-voting-your-voice-gender-equity-makes-difference/84861.

Sargent, Thomas J. (n.d.) *"Rational Expectations."* Available at: www.econlib.org/library/Enc/RationalExpectations.html.

Schwartz, Hugh. (2002) "Herbert Simon and Behavioral Economics," *The Journal of Socio-Economics*, 31(2).

Schmidt, C. & Undark (2020) "Coronavirus Researchers TriedTo Warn Us," *The Atlantic.*

Segal, J. (2015) "New SSGA Ron O'Hanley Says Asset Allocation Is the New Active," *Institutional Investor.*

Serafeim, G. & Yoon, A. (2020) "Does the Market React to Corporate ESG News," Working Paper (advance copy provided to authors).

Sheffrin, Stephen M. (1996) *Rational Expectations.* (2nd ed., Cambridge Survey of Economic Literature). Cambridge: Cambridge University Press.

Silk D. & Niles, S, (2018) "Department of Labor Cautionary Tone on ESG-Related Activities," Blog, Harvard Law School Forum on Corporate Governance. Available at: https://corpgov.law.harvard.edu/2018/05/02/department-of-labor-cautionary-tone-on-esg-related-activities.

Skancke, M. (2010) *The Government Pension Fund Global and the Management of Petroleum Wealth.* Oslo: Norwegian Ministry of Finance.

Smith, Adam. (1790) *The Theory of Moral Sentiments* (1759, revised 1790). Available at: www.econlib.org/library/Smith/smMS.html?chapter_num=2#book-reader.

Stringer, S. (2014) "NYC Pension Funds Launch National Campaign To Give Shareowners A True Voice In How Corporate Boards Are Elected," New York City Comptroller Office Press Release.

Stych, A. (2019) "Women's representation on boards reaches a milestone," *Bizwomen.*

Sullivan, Rodney N. & Xiong, James X. (2012) "How Index Trading Increases Market Vulnerability," *Financial Analysts Journal*, 68(2): 70–84.

Suzuki, Hirofumi. (2015) "Comovement and index fund trading effect: evidence from the Japanese stock market," *Economics Bulletin, AccessEcon*, 35(2), 949–958.

Taleb, Nassim. (2007) *The Black Swan.* New York, NY: Random House.

Thompson, Clive. (2017) "When Robots Take All of Our Jobs, Remember the Luddites," *Smithsonian Magazine* (January). Available at: www.smithsonianmag.com/innovation/when-robots-take-jobs-remember-luddites-180961423.

Truvalue Labs. (2019) "Dynamic Materiality: Measuring what matters." Available at: https://insights.truvaluelabs.com/white-paper/dynamic-materiality-download.

United Press International. (1984) "Quaker State Buys Back Shares from Steinberg," *United Press International.*

Useem, Michael & Hess, David. (2001) "Governance and Investment of Public Pensions," chapter 7 in Mitchell, Olivia S. & Hustead, Edwin (eds), *Pensions in the Public Sector.* Philadelphia, PA: University of Pennsylvania Press.

van Dillen, J.G.; Poitras, G.; & Majithia, A. (2006), "Isaac LeMaire and the early trading in Dutch East India Company Shares," *Pioneers of Financial Economics*, Volume 1. London: Edward Elgar Publishing.

Van Heeckeren, J. (1997) "Managers' Journal; Why Investors Push for Strong Corporate Boards," *Asian Wall Street Journal.*

Vise, D.A. (1985) "Bill of Rights Seeks to Boost Power of Shareholders," *The Washington Post.*

William, Watts. (2020) "S&P 500 tumbles from record finish to correction in just 6 trading days as stock-market rout accelerates," *MarketWatch*, (February 28). Available at: www. marketwatch.com/story/dow-sp-500-enter-correction-territory-as-stock-market-selloff-rolls -on-for-6th-straight-day-2020-02-27.

Williamson, Oliver E. (1993) "Transaction cost economics and organizational theory,", *Industry and corporate change*, (2)2: 107–156. Available at: www.researchgate.net/pro-file/Oliver_Williamson3/publication/31462357_Transaction_Cost_Economics_and_Orga nization_Theory/links/5655fd8c08ae1ef92979be1e.pdf.

Williamson, Oliver E. (2000) "The New Institutional Economics: Taking Stock, Looking Ahead," *Journal of Economic Literature*, 38(3): 595–613.

Williamson, Oliver E. (2007) "Transaction cost economics: an introduction," Economics Discussion Papers, No. 2007–2003, Kiel Institute for the World Economy (IfW), Kiel. Available at: www.econstor.eu/bitstream/10419/17926/1/dp2007-3.pdf.

Williamson, Oliver E. (2008) "Transaction cost economics," in Ménardé, Claude & Shirley, Mary M. *Handbook of New Institutional Economics* (Springer). Available at: https://studfile.net/preview/5714480/page:5.

West, J. and Pickard, A. (2019) "Plausible Performance: Have Smart Beta Return Claims Jumped the Shark?", *Research Affiliates*. Available at: www.researchaffiliates.com/ en_us/publications/articles/767-plausible-performance.html?evar36=eml_plausible-perfor mance-hero-title&_cldee=amx1a29tbmlrQHNpbmNsYWlyY2FwaXRhbC5jb20%3d&r ecipientid=contact-2880b5f8c7cbe2119aa7005056bc3cff-42a2b5dbe4e24286ab95ff52b9ed2 4a9&esid=b3728812-e715-ea11-80e4-f24e75708764.

Wiener-Bronner, D. (2017) "Why a defiant girl is staring down the Wall Street bull, " CNN Money.

Wilde, Oscar. (1892) *Lady Windemere's Fan*.

World Economic Forum (in collaboration with Boston Consulting Group). (2020) "Embra-cing the New Age of Materiality; Harnessing the pace of change in ESG." March.

Wurgler, J. (2010) "On the economic consequences of index-linked investing," NBER Working Paper No.16376. Available at: https://www.nber.org/papers/w16376.

Index

Page numbers in italics refer to figures. Page numbers followed by 'n' refer to notes.